EXMOOR
— *40 YEARS ON*

written by
HILARY BINDING

FOR THE EXMOOR NATIONAL PARK AUTHORITY

IN CELEBRATION OF THE FIRST FORTY YEARS OF

THE EXMOOR NATIONAL PARK

*PHOTOGRAPHIC RESEARCH
AND ADVICE*
MICHAEL DEERING

EXMOOR BOOKS

© Hilary Binding

First published in 1994

EXMOOR BOOKS
Dulverton, Somerset

Trade sales enquiries:
Westcountry Books
Halsgrove House
Lower Moor Way
Tiverton EX16 6SS

Tel: (0884) 243242
Fax: (0884) 243325

*Exmoor Books is a Partnership between
The Exmoor Press and The Exmoor National Park Authority*

British Library Cataloguing in Publication Data
A CIP Catalogue Record for this book is
available from the British Library

ISBN 0 86183 271 X

Cover illustration: *Sheep on Brendon Common* (Brian Pearce)
Inset: *Winsford Sheep Fair, early 1930s*

Printed in Great Britain by
Longdunn Press, Bristol

Contents

Pinkery Pond.

Preface

It is forty years since Exmoor became a National Park. Although it is a time for looking to the future it is also salutary to look back to see how much Exmoor has altered within living memory.

This book, commissioned by the Exmoor National Park Authority to mark the fortieth anniversary, is a celebration of Exmoor itself. In it, the changes which have taken place are brought to life in photographs and the reminiscences of many people who saw those changes happen.

The old photographs have been collected from many local people and form part of a photographic archive of Exmoor being put together by Michael Deering for the Exmoor National Park Authority. They are just the tip of the iceberg! Attempts to take views from exactly the same point have not always been possible. The foot of the Brendon Hill Incline is shrouded in trees while at Wimbleball an underwater camera would be needed! Nonetheless the contrasting modern photographs, in comparison with the old, convey the essence of the changes.

This book would not have been possible without the support of many, many people who have shared not only their photographs but their memories. They represent the people of Exmoor. This book is dedicated to them.

Fetching water at Winsford c.1900.

Introduction

Nothing on earth ever stays the same. The face of Exmoor that we know and love today has been formed over thousands of years, partly by natural forces, wind, rain, the crashing waves against the shore, but also by the impact of people going about their ordinary, everyday affairs. This century has seen more dramatic changes than any other and those changes have reached into every aspect of our lives.

For people on Exmoor change came slowly. The area was often described by visitors as being twenty, forty, even fifty years behind the times. It was a part of its charm. Even now, isolated properties out on the moor are without mains electricity, power provided by a generator housed in a barn. Others rely on water piped straight into the house from a nearby spring that has not run dry since the site was first settled more than a thousand years ago.

During the last fifty years, as elsewhere, the pace of change has quickened; agriculture has intensified; traffic increased in volume and speed; many local people now work away from the moor while others from outside, seeking the peace and tranquillity that Exmoor offers, have bought second homes or moved to live in the area. Visitors now drive hundreds of miles in a day for a brief glimpse of Exmoor's hills

and coast. The Exmoor fashioned slowly over thousands of years by the quiet husbandry of men and women living close to the soil, has become subject to the pressures of modern living and its fragile environment, home to a multitude of living things, has been threatened.

Without some sort of protection the peace and quiet beauty of Exmoor could have been lost for ever. The whole moor might have been ploughed up, covered in conifers or parts even turned into a gigantic theme park. When Exmoor was designated a National Park in 1954 many people wondered why. They did not dispute the beauty of the landscape but failed to see that intensified agriculture and recreation might bring alterations in the use of the land which could lead to the destruction of the Exmoor they knew and loved.

This book is about Exmoor during the last seventy years and some of the changes that have taken place particularly since it became a National Park. Many people whose families have lived and worked on Exmoor for generations have lent photographs, shared memories and told me anecdotes of the years before and since Exmoor became a National Park. Their love of Exmoor and their wish to retain its beauty and its secrets to share with others is also the wish of Exmoor National Park Authority.

View over Malmsmead from County Gate.

EXMOOR:
'a landscape of enduring beauty but with a changing face'

Near Mole's Chamber c.1948.

Left: *Near Mole's Chamber 1994.*
Above: *A mock-up of the radar station proposed for a site near Shoulsbury Castle.*

There are many parts of Exmoor where the face of the landscape has altered little over the last half century. Here, at an isolated spot some five miles from Challacombe, the only real change seems to be the replacement of the tumble-down five-bar gate by a hunting gate. The grass moorland, the hedges, the wire fence posts, all remain the same. In the background, the 'haerepath', thought by some to have been used by the Saxon army, marches up over the hill as it has done for a thousand years or more.

But every place is vulnerable.

In 1985 a consortium including the Meteorological Office, South West Water and Devon County Council applied for permission to build a radar weather station, to be one of a network involved in short-term forecasting of 'precipitation', close to Shoulsbury Castle, the site of an Iron Age hill-fort less than a mile to the south-west of Mole's Chamber. An earlier application to build a radar station on Five Barrows had been rejected by Exmoor National Park Authority but the consortium insisted that a moorland site was essential. Planning permission was refused by the Park Committee. After an Inquiry the Inspector recommended approval but the Secretary of State for the Environment (Nicholas Ridley) disagreed and turned down the scheme describing it as 'inappropriate, intrusive and likely to have adverse environmental effects'. On this occasion a blatant threat to landscape was averted.

Above: *Shoulsbarrow Farm from Rocky Lane 1945.* Below: *Shoulsbarrow Farm, the same view 1992.*

Shoulsbarrow Farm

Only two miles from Mole's Chamber as the crow flies, lies Shoulsbarrow Farm, occupied and worked by the Dallyn family for more than 250 years. In the *Exmoor Review* of 1994, George Huxtable described the farm's 360 acres as 'an area of rich contrasts: high moorland, wet moor, sunken lanes, deep attractive combes and superb beech hedges built to provide welcome shade in summertime and shelter from winter storms.' Its varied habitats supported rarities ranging from the bee orchid to club moss and the air was vibrant with the heady scent of flowers, the rushing of the mill stream and the calling of the curlew. Rocky Lane, leading to the open moor, was 'a rock garden on the grand scale'.

By 1990 the farm and 2000 acres of land round Challacombe had passed to a new owner whose vision of a contemporary farm estate providing employment for the people of the area did not include the care of this tranquil and traditional landscape. To accommodate modern building equipment and up-to-date farming methods and machinery drastic measures were needed. Rocky Lane was filled in and the beech hedges destroyed; field boundaries were removed and the wet moor drained; even the shapes of the valleys themselves were altered while the old farmhouse was left standing, isolated and gaunt, with no sheltering belt of trees.

This did not happen overnight and local people watched in sadness and anger. The National Park Authority whose planning powers are limited to basic planning permission, the protection of listed buildings and tree preservation, could do nothing until the new owner applied for planning permission to renovate and extend the farmhouse and barns as a house for a farm-manager. Then, anxious for the well-being of the site, they took action, refusing the application on the grounds 'that the scale of the proposed dwelling and its man-made grounds would be an unacceptable visual intrusion into this attractive area' and would therefore be in conflict with their statutory duty of preserving and enhancing the natural beauty of Exmoor National Park. By then of course, the worst of the damage was done.

The case of Shoulsbarrow Farm arose from a clash of interests and attitudes. The new owner of the farm saw himself as a saviour of the area in the mould of John and Frederic Knight who had reclaimed and enclosed Exmoor for farming in the first part of the nineteenth century. But attitudes have changed and care for the vanishing countryside has now to be considered alongside exploitation of the land. Balancing the needs of the countryside itself with those of the working community - and of tourism - is the National Park Authority's prime responsibility which it tries to carry out with sensitivity as well as firmness.

Hoaroak Hill on the Chains.

Beginnings

The wooded Exmoor coast at Woody Bay.

The hanging Woods, that touch'd by Autumn seem'd
As they were blossoming hues of fire & gold,
The hanging Woods, most lovely in decay,
The many clouds, the Sea, the Rocks, the Sand
Lay in the silent moonshine - and the Owl,
(Strange, very strange!) the Scritch-owl only wak'd,
Sole Voice, sole Eye of all that world of Beauty!

S. T. Coleridge
from *Osorio*

The poet, William Wordsworth, is often given the credit for being the first person to have the idea of setting aside beautiful, wild areas of countryside for people to enjoy. In his 'Guide to the Lakes' which was published in 1810, he wrote, 'The Lakes are a sort of national property in which every man has a right and interest, who has an eye to perceive and a heart to enjoy.'

Some twelve years earlier, when living at Alfoxden House near Holford in the foothills of the Quantocks, William and his sister Dorothy were introduced to Exmoor by his friend and fellow poet, Samuel Taylor Coleridge. Together they took long walks along the coast to Lynton and the Valley of Rocks and inland to Dulverton, delighting in the romantic scenery of mountain, cliff, wood and water. It was at this time that attitudes towards the countryside began to change. What had been seen simply as a working environment was now beginning to be regarded as something to be valued for its own sake.

It was to be nearly a century and a half before the most beautiful, wild areas of countryside in England and Wales were made into National Parks and given special protection under the law so that they would be there for everyone to enjoy for all time. The development of the concept of National Parks and the movement towards setting them up was complex and piecemeal. It had its roots not just in the romanticism of writers and artists but more pragmatically, in a reaction to the effects of the industrial revolution which swept the country in the first part of the nineteenth century. Thousands of people moved from the country to live and work in new industrial towns. As these towns grew and more land was enclosed,

both for building and for increased farming to feed the growing population, the amount of open land available for use by ordinary people for recreation and relaxation declined drastically. Commons were fenced off, footpaths stopped up, moor and heath put under the plough and in some of the larger cities even disused graveyards were sold for building plots.

As people began to take up these issues, three main concerns emerged. Firstly, that the access to open areas, which people living in the country formerly took for granted, was being limited; secondly, that people's health and well-being suffered if they had no opportunity for recreation and relaxation in the open air and finally, concern for the preservation of the landscape itself. These three issues, access, recreation and conservation, were to be raised and discussed and fought over again and again until after the second world war when, in 1949, the National Parks and Access to the Countryside Act was passed .

On Exmoor, as in other places, open land began to disappear during the nineteenth century. Some thirty commons were lost between 1841 and 1872 while wide tracts of the old Royal Forest were enclosed for farmland with approval all round. There was still so much open moorland that there can have been little long-term impact on wildlife and most people must have continued to work and have access to the land as they had always done, but perhaps it was no coincidence that the first large gift of open land to the National Trust was of part of Exmoor. Those Exmoor landowners who rode for pleasure over the open moor may well have recognised in the nineteenth century movement towards moorland reclamation for farming, the possibility that without some protection the moorland might be lost. Some, like the Acland family, had long been concerned that people should have opportunities to walk and enjoy the beauty of the Exmoor landscape.

In 1910, Octavia Hill, one of those people who had been concerned with the decline of open space and a co-founder of the National Trust, visited Minehead and walked on North Hill, coming down 'the hillside by a lovely path cut on the slope by Sir Thos. Acland who also has made innumerable lovely paths, all thro' his woods, all open to the public'.

'It's really a magnificent stretch of country. Jolly to think it'll all be national.'
Francis Acland in a letter to his wife, Eleanor. 22 February 1917.

Dunkery Hill

On 22 February, 1917, the Earl of Plymouth, Chairman of the Executive Committee of the National Trust, announced in a letter to the Editor of *The Times* the gift (actually a 500 year lease) by Sir Thomas Acland of Killerton (in Devon) and Holnicote (near Selworthy) of some 8000 acres of Exmoor so that they might be 'permanently preserved in their natural condition.' In his letter Lord Plymouth wrote: 'Most of your readers know that Exmoor is one of the most beautiful of the few wild places in England which circumstances have allowed to remain almost in their original condition.' Sir Thomas (Charlie) Acland took this initiative 'a generation ahead of his time'. The land included some of the best loved heather moorland of Exmoor, 'a great part of the valleys of Horner and Sweetworthy, which lie under Dunkery Beacon... as well as the farm at Cloutsham' and 'the wilder parts of North Hill, which runs down to Hurtstone Point, in the Bristol Channel, and a stretch of wild moorland on Winsford Hill, north-west of Dulverton between the rivers Exe and Barle, including the very ancient causeway over the Barle known as Tarr Steps.'(In fact Tarr Steps was never owned by the National Trust.)

At the time, the whole property, 'one of very varied beauty, including hill and valley, woodland and bare moor', was the largest and most interesting property yet offered to the Trust and it was hoped that the generous and far-seeing spirit which had moved Sir Thomas to make the offer would prove an example 'to other owners anxious to safeguard the places they have known and loved.'

On Exmoor it did. In 1932, the same year that the mass trespass of hikers on Kinder Scout, in the Peak District, focussed attention on the need for public access to open countryside, Colonel Walter Wiggins presented 860 acres on Dunkery Hill to the National Trust. Two years later, Mrs Allan Hughes gave 945 acres which included the top of Dunkery Beacon. Then, in 1944, the lease made by his great-uncle in 1917 was converted by Sir Richard Acland into an outright gift of the whole of the Holnicote Estate to the National Trust, partly as a matter of principle that land should be owned commonly but also to preserve the estate intact for future generations.

Unveiling the plaque commemorating gifts of land on Dunkery Hill to the National Trust 1937.

Coronation Beacon on Dunkery 1937.

Even before 1938 when the well-respected local photographer, Alfred Vowles, wrote his guide to Dunkery, the conflict between preservation of landscape and enjoyment by all was apparent on Exmoor. Vowles estimated that 'thousands of people ascend Dunkery each season' while the footpath from Dunkery Hill Gate to Dunkery Beacon was already between three and four feet wide, 'bare and stony'.

The summit was once topped by three cairns, the ruins of 'splendid hilltop tumuli' (burial mounds) but the removal of stones for various purposes, the trampling of others into the ground and the deliberate uprooting of large stones just for the fun of it in the autumn of 1938 had damaged this archaeological site beyond repair. Vowles comments on the lack of guidance and control which might have prevented this happening.

The bonfire on Dunkery Beacon, built to celebrate the coronation of George VI and Queen Elizabeth in 1937, was the biggest ever seen on Exmoor and was reported fully in the local Press. A crowd, five thousand strong, came to Dunkery in a thousand motor vehicles, from most parts of Somerset and Devon. The stack of 'more than a thousand logs and faggots' stood over forty feet high and was beflagged and floodlit. One hundred torch bearers processed round the summit, led by an accordion band in oriental costume. The flames leapt in a 'fiery storm to heaven' and the moor around glowed in ruddy, flickering light. (Not so in 1977, when on the occasion of Queen Elizabeth II's Silver Jubilee celebrations, the mist came down and watchers on Porlock Hill, hoping to see beacon light from Dunkery, Selworthy and the Brecon Beacons, saw nothing!)

The cairn on the summit of Dunkery Hill before restoration work began. A careful comparison with the photograph of the unveiling ceremony indicates the extent of erosion.

Nowadays thousands of people climb or ride on horseback to the summit of Dunkery Hill every year, each set of feet wearing away a little more of the hillside and widening the footpaths as they search out the easiest route to the top. In 1991 it became apparent from photographic and other evidence, that the ground level around the cairn at the very top of the Beacon had been worn away so much that it was 28 inches lower than it was in 1937. To prevent any further deterioration of the site, the National Trust decided that this dramatic landmark must be restored. In 1993, 150 tons of large stone, quarried at Timberscombe, and 150 tons of smaller material that had been washed down from the moor by rivers,

The cairn after restoration work was completed 1993.

were taken by earth-moving vehicles with inflatable tyres, to the top of the hill. Large rocks were used to under-pin the cairn and then were placed jig-saw fashion over the summit, smaller material being used to fill the gaps and make a level surface. Now the summit of the Beacon is, once again, 1704' above sea level.

Footpath erosion on Dunkery Hill 1993.

Aerial view of Dunkery Hill showing eroded footpaths.

This bird's eye view of Dunkery Hill shows the white lines of eroded footpaths criss-crossing the moor and leading to the summit. The problem of footpaths wearing away is common to all National Parks and popular beauty spots and quite a lot of work has been done to develop techniques for restoring upland paths. Recently the National Trust and the Park Authority have started to work together on the Dunkery Project. Specialists in the problems of footpath erosion have been employed to investigate the footpaths in the Dunkery area and to work out the best ways of restoring them and limiting future damage. Work on restoration has begun and the techniques that prove most successful here will eventually be used on other parts of Exmoor.

Outside the Lion Hotel at Dulverton c.1905.

Left: *Recording the evidence.*
Below: *Outside the Exmoor Forest Hotel, Simonsbath, 1906. This vehicle is said to have been the first car seen on Exmoor.*

The Valley of Rocks c.1950.
A sign of things to come.

The Valley of Rocks c.1990.

Florence Hall, Landgirl.

Florence Hall was parlourmaid to Sir Edward and Lady Malet at Chargot at Luxborough until she joined the Women's Land Army in 1942. On her first day she was taken to moorland on the top of Elworthy Barrows on the Brendons. 'It was pouring with rain, cold and a dense fog. We were given staff hooks and were told to cut the heather and gorse bushes off at ground level. This was very tough work. Blisters appeared on our hands and we soon found out where our muscles were. We had to dig the small thorn bushes out but tractors were used to pull out the larger bushes. All the bush stuff had to be burnt and cleared away because a special wide plough (which we called a Prairie Buster) was used to plough up this moorland and there was great activity with us cutting and burning, followed by the plough, rollers and cultivators and then rollers again.'

They planted the whole area with potatoes to break up the virgin soil and then moved on to do similar work on other moorland on the Brendons. 'The second year the moor was ready for corn sowing.'

Fine crops of cereals were harvested on the hills for just two years in the war following exceptional summers but then bad weather made harvesting impossible. The demands of the War Agricultural Committee (generally known as the War Ag.) caused annoyance and frustration to many of Exmoor's farmers, compelled to plant cereals and potatoes on land they knew to be unsuitable. As John Stoate, local spokesman for the National Farmers' Union, said, 'On the hills you have the best views and the poorest harvesting. Hundreds of acres of corn on our hill-country have not been cut and never will be because it is impossible. We are not against ploughing up orders, but we are concerned at being told to grow corn in areas which are not suitable.' It was only after the corn harvest failed that farmers were encouraged instead to improve their land for grass and food for livestock, something which some would continue to do, with Government help, when the war was over.

The Chains.

What would the world be, once bereft
Of wet and of wildness? Let them be left,
O let them be left, wildness and wet;
Long live the weeds and the wilderness yet.

Gerard Manley Hopkins
from *Inversnaid*

It was during the dark days of the war with all its anxieties and pressures that the movement towards National Parks in England and Wales gained momentum. Dreams and visions of a better Britain after the war were given substance as one after another, government surveys and reports tackled the issues of urbanisation, rural planning, nature conservation, recreation, access and National Parks. In April 1945 John Dower produced his masterly report, *National Parks in England and Wales*, which defined the scope and nature of National Parks, suggested suitable areas, outlined a system of administration and examined problems. When the Labour Party was swept to power soon after, the issues were considered sympathetically and a committee was appointed under the chairmanship of Arthur Hobhouse, to examine the implementation of the Report.

On Exmoor there seems to have been little obvious interest at the time in the possibility that Exmoor might become a National Park. In spite of the concerns of landowners and the resulting gifts to the National Trust, the growing number of visitors and the encouragement of agricultural development during the war, it was not apparent to most local people that the Exmoor they knew and loved was beginning to disappear. E. W. Hendy, the naturalist, thought that if Exmoor became a National Park it would become some kind of huge nature reserve where all animals would be protected and hunting forbidden. (He was thinking especially of the red deer and not the Exmoor pony, which, at the time he was writing, 1942, was near extinction).

In the Hobhouse Report of 1947 Exmoor was named as one of twelve possible National Parks. 'Exmoor is one of the smallest proposed National Parks with an area of 318 square miles but bounded on the north by 29 miles of exceptionally beautiful coast.' From its highest point, the seventeen hundred foot Dunkery Beacon commands extensive views. 'Much of Exmoor's fine heather, bracken and grass moorland rises to between 1000' and 1500'. The whole plateau is seamed with combes, many well wooded with scrub oak, birch, mountain ash and alder, others sheltering big timber trees - oak, ash, walnut and various conifers. Gnarled and weather-beaten thorns are studded about the moorlands, and well grown beech hedges border many of the lanes and upland pastures.'

The proposed boundary included the Quantocks (which were eventually to be left out of the Park), and the Brendon Hills with their richly wooded valleys and patches of rough common land and heather. 'A fine ridge road runs the whole length of the Brendons from Elworthy to Wheddon Cross and the motorist, the cyclist and the walker can satisfy his taste for quiet exploration in the intricate network of smaller roads and inviting country lanes which lead from one hidden village to another through a countryside of great beauty. There are good roads, many bridle-paths and tracks and access is practically unrestricted.'

Exmoor appeared to the Hobhouse Committee as 'a potential National Park which is happily free from serious problems. The Service Departments make no demands upon its land for military training, water catchment schemes and mineral workings are few and unobtrusive and a large part of the area is already under the protection of the National Trust.'

EXMOOR NATIONAL PARK
ORDER SIGNED

Now Subject to Confirmation by Minister

CHAIRMAN OF COMMISSION GIVES REASONS

DESPITE opposition from Somerset and Devon County Councils
and supported by rural district councils in the area, the chairman
of the National Parks Commission (Sir Patrick Duff) on Wednesday
signed the Exmoor National Park (Designation) Order. This is the
eighth National Park to be designated.

The Order will be submitted in due course to the Minister of Housing
and Local Government for confirmation. The effect of the Order when
confirmed by the Minister is to constitute the land to which it relates
a National Park.

The area comprises a total of about 265 square miles of which 77 are
in Devon and 188 in Somerset.

West Somerset Free Press, *extract 30 January 1954.*

The main possible problem seemed to be the planting of conifers especially on Croydon Hill near Dunster. Future planting, they suggested, should be mixed wherever possible to 'perpetuate the original beauty and variety of the Exmoor woodlands.' It was the threat of conifer planting on the Chains, a wild, bare region of wet grass moorland, that brought the conservation and pressure group, the Exmoor Society, into being and it is interesting that even now, the Park Authority has no powers to prevent a landowner from planting regimented conifers if he wants to.

Other potential problems included the high beech hedges which 'sometimes obstruct the view for long distances. Specially fine views from frequented roads might be opened up by occasional trimming down or by breaking the continuous line of hedges or banks and replacing them with suitable fencing.' The widespread use of corrugated iron as a cheap roofing material for barns and even houses was condemned

Beech hedge.

Exford Youth Hostel was opened in 1965. The property was bought by Somerset County Council and sold to the Youth Hostel Association for £10 as part of the National Park Committee's commitment to providing more accommodation for young people and riders. The Hostel was the main pony-trekking centre on the moor for many years. The stables have since been sold.

and Committtee members also noted that more accommodation was needed on the moor as well as stabling for riders and hostels for walkers.

In 1954 Exmoor was designated a National Park, the eighth to be set up. But it was not to be all plain sailing. Both Devon and Somerset County Councils, together with the Rural District Councils, were opposed to Exmoor becoming a National Park. They were sure that they would be able to preserve the natural beauty of Exmoor and provide for recreation just as well as any specially set up body which would no doubt mean an increase in the rates.

At the Inquiry held in June 1954, Sir Patrick Duff (Chairman of the National Parks Commission) replied to these objections. 'We regard Exmoor, with its lovely and majestic scenery, its renown, its romance, its extent and fascinating wild landscape as eminently falling in with the idea and the terms prescribed by Parliament for National Parks.'

'If the National Parks Act means anything at all, and if the whole National Parks idea means anything, Exmoor is a National Park.'

The objectors were over-ruled.

It was to be three years before Devon and Somerset set up committees with reponsibility for looking after the Park, one for each county, and a Joint Advisory Committee. It was not until 1974, as a result of a new Local Government Act, that a single and separate National Park Department was established with a chief officer, a skeleton staff and offices at Exmoor House in Dulverton.

Exmoor House, once the Union Workhouse, administrative centre of the Exmoor National Park Authority since 1974.

Dulverton Ancient Order of Foresters meeting outside
Exmoor House c.1907.

The Land

Larkbarrow Farm c.1900.

Larkbarrow

Larkbarrow - the calling
When the bird rang out
Small and fixed in the sky
I rejoiced (to have the name live so)

But only a half:

What of the mound
That lay dark
Of its own shadow?

Barry Darch
Exmoor Review

Larkbarrow Farm 1994.

Larkbarrow - a microcosm of Exmoor

The ruins of Larkbarrow Farm stand, shrouded by trees and shrub, at the centre of a bare and open landscape. Coming from the Porlock Road to Alderman's Barrow, close to where the old track from Exford to Larkbarrow Farm crosses the highway, the first sudden glimpse of this wide, white expanse of grass moorland is startling, causing the breath to catch and the heart to leap. The flat-topped hills encompass the walker while high above, the larks soar and sing. The place was aptly named, though the nearby Lark Barrow has long gone.

The area around Larkbarrow is a microcosm of the central Exmoor plateau and the whole history of the high moorland is reflected in this place. Some eight thousand years ago the hills were covered with trees and shrub and occupied in summer by nomadic hunters wandering in search of food. Nearby, at Hawkcombe Head, skilled men worked flint to make

The ruins of Larkbarrow Farm 1994.

sharp arrowheads and tools and left scatterings of chippings to mark the spot. Tracks passing close by were routes for traders, linking the area with ports on the North Devon coast and with the Somerset Levels.

More settled farmers of the Neolithic and Bronze Age period began to cut down the trees for timber, used in buildings and fencing, for artefacts and for fuel. Small fields were enclosed and cultivated, while animals were put to graze on the cleared ground. The weather was warmer and people made greater use of the moor for grazing, setting up stones to mark holy places and burying their dead under the great heaps of stone and earth that we know as barrows. Whether the Lark Barrow was such a burial mound or simply a heap of stones to mark the later Forest boundary is not certain.

The Saxons settled on lower ground where there was protection and water while the wild centre of the moor, outside (foras) the jurisdiction of the villages, was held by the crown for hunting and became known as the Royal Forest of Exmoor. The Lark Barrow lay on the forest boundary that separated the forest from the commons used by villagers for grazing, cutting peat and gathering fuel.

There was some hunting in the forest during the medieval period but more important to the economy of the area was its extensive use for summer grazing of sheep and cattle which were put on the moor from spring until autumn. In the winter only the indigenous Exmoor ponies were able to survive the harshness of the weather on the high moorland.

Little changed in the use of the Forest over centuries but from 1508 it was leased for a fixed rent to a Warden who was free to make what money he could from grazing and other uses while at the same time enjoying the hunting. During the Commonwealth the Forest was sold by Parliament to a former tenant, James Boevey. He was an unusual man, a writer and thinker, determined to maintain all his rights on

Exmoor against the claims of local farmers, however many lawsuits it involved. It is said that he kept candle, pen and paper beside his bed so that if he woke in the night with a new idea he could jot it down rather than lose it.

After the restoration of the monarchy the Forest reverted to the crown and to the policy of leasing until, in the early nineteenth century during the Napoleonic Wars when food was short, it was decided that the ancient forest should be sold for agricultural reclamation and be enclosed. In 1818, John Knight, an iron master from Wolverley in Worcestershire with an interest in farming change, bought much of the Forest for £50, 000.

One of the first things that John Knight had to do was to enclose his new estate and a section of the wall, built for this purpose, was later to form part of the boundary of Larkbarrow Farm. He soon set about reclaiming land, starting with that on the south-facing slopes of the River Barle, spading, ploughing and liming ground that had never been cultivated before. His attempts to run the whole estate from one central point were not really successful and, on taking over the estate in 1841, his son Frederic began to build new farms for leasing to tenants.

Larkbarrow Farm was put up in 1846 during the second phase of building and was let to 'old Farmer Hayes of Exford' who continued to live at Exford and ran Larkbarrow from there, perhaps wisely, since he gave up the tenancy after only two years.

In 1849, Larkbarrow Farm was let again, this time to James Meadows from Leicestershire, who began enthusiastically to clear the ground for roots and rotation grasses, and if rumour is to be believed, even a crop of wheat. A fine Stilton cheese produced with milk from his herd of Red Devons gained a rapid reputation for excellence but his success was short-lived. In his account of twelve years on Exmoor, William Hannam, the dispirited tenant of Cornham, wrote: 'Mr Meadows took on Lark B Farm after Fr Hays and a conciderable deal more to it I believe to the Extent of 900 Acres - Mr Meadows comenced to buy in a lott of Steers and verey good Cattle in May and June from the Inland Contreys up to the number of 70 or 80. He had no Land or verey little that had bin nearley seeded out and his Land in general was produsing verey indiferent pasture. the stock was going back in Condition instead of Forward and not having a provision for the winter was oblidged to sell them in the Autom at a great sacrifice.'

Meadows persevered until 1852 when he admitted defeat and gave up the tenancy. 'The Lark Barrow Farm no one has Taken since Mr Meadows leaved it. I think in the end Mr Knight will see it is not a lott of Gentleman Farmers that live maney Milles away is going to improve it much but are more likeley to bring some of the old Mens words True that they should see it Exmoor again and as before a sheep walk and the Farm Houses occupied by Shepperds and Herdman.'

Frederic Knight was soon to recognise the unsuitability of Exmoor for lowland styles of farming and by the later 1860s sheep ranching had been re-introduced across much of the high moorland. Scottish Blackface sheep were run on the Larkbarrow herding, tended during the 1860s and '70s by William and Adam Dunn from Northumberland, then by the Scottish shepherd, Thomas Graham, and later by members of the Little family living at Tom's Hill nearby. By this time the estate had been sold to the Fortescue family who continued the run sheep (Cheviots) on the open moor.

From 1898 the Larkbarrow farmhouse took on a different role being let as a hunting and shooting box together with extensive sporting rights over the moor. It was perhaps occupied in this way on a day in the 1920s when Mr Archie Galliford of Barnstaple, out walking on the moor, called at the house to ask for a

A section of the wall built by John Knight before 1824 to enclose his Exmoor estate. Here, near Larkbarrow, it is easy to distinguish between the heather and grass moorland on either side of the wall, the result of different management practices.

glass of milk and was astonished to be received by a butler in frock coat and white gloves!

Larkbarrow Farm continued to be let for hunting or holidays until the Second World War when the farm and Tom's Hill were requisitioned as a site for artillery practice and most of the buildings were destroyed. The farmhouse itself was finally ruined by American soldiers, camped nearby on Gallon House allotment and with little to do, who used it for target practice. The ground was not finally cleared of ammunition until the early 1980s as part of the preparations by the Park Authority to allow more public access.

In 1981 Larkbarrow Farm was put up for sale as a property ripe for 'improvement'. This would have meant rebuilding the house and 'improving' the land for stock with consequent loss of moorland. To prevent this happening the National Park Authority, with financial help from central government, bought the farm with the intention of conserving rather than improving the land while at the same time opening it up to the public.

In the past, continuous heavy grazing and annual burning at Larkbarrow, as well as some liming, have prevented the re-growth of many plants so that purple moor grass has become dominant and the varied colours and textures of heather moorland have been lost. The idea behind the Authority's current management of the land is, by controlled grazing and burning, to increase the diversity of plant life which should lead to an increased variety of habitats.

Frank Burnell ploughing at Westermill, Exford, c.1938.

Haymaking, Cloggs Farm, Hawkridge 1947.
Family, workmen and visitors help to get in the hay.

'The end of a perfect day.'

A sled being used to transport hay at Brandish Street, near Allerford.
Sleds were used widely on the moor before roads were improved.

Left: *Alfie with his scythe at Selworthy c.1900.*
Below: *Baling hay 1992.*

Snapshots from the albums of the Bawden family, Cloggs Farm, Hawkridge. 1936–1954.

Exmoor Horn Sheep are, like Devon Closewools, a hardy breed indigenous to Exmoor.

Many farmers kept a house cow to provide milk and butter for family use.

Red Devons, the native Exmoor breed.

The children had their part to play in the life of the farm.

Off to the fields.

Sunny snapshots disguise the fact that for the Exmoor hill-farmer fifty years or so ago, making a living was hard physical work, seven days a week, and for many, a constant struggle to make ends meet. The years between the two world wars were particularly difficult for farmers everywhere, not least on Exmoor.

One farmer's daughter living out at Challacombe recorded in her diary for 1927 the quantities of butter she and her sister made each week. She recalls how they took it by pony and trap to the Pannier Market at Barnstaple accompanied by dire warnings from their mother that they must return with at least thirty shillings (£1.50) to pay the men's wages. Many farmers' wives supplemented their income by letting rooms to visitors or 'London folk', as they were sometimes called, their own families squashing up together to make room. There were a few wealthier farmers with capital but they were the exception.

The Second World War was in one way a blessing in disguise for Exmoor's hill-farmers who were now encouraged to produce as much food on their land as they possibly could and were given grants by the War Ag. to help them do so. After the war the subsidies continued encouraging farmers to produce as much food as possible by reviving and making full use of all their land and keeping larger numbers of sheep and cattle. In order to feed the increased stock some farmers looked to improving their land by ploughing, fertilising and re-seeding and the government encouraged this by paying half the cost of converting moorland to grass.

When the Mass Observation Unit visited Luccombe in 1946, they recorded that 'Mr Westcott of Wilmersham Farm in the parish of Stoke Pero' had recently put twenty-four acres of heather under the plough. 'Mr Westcott says that many of his neighbours are laughing at him for taking the trouble to cultivate this rough land but he has high hopes that before too long he will be able to prove to them that his trouble has not been in vain. It is puzzling to know why many farmers are loath to plough up rough land now that the War Agricultural Committee has brought the necessary machinery to them. It is not a new experiment, for it was done half a century ago on the waste land around Simonsbath by the late Sir Frederic Knight.' The barren waste and rough land referred to were grass and heather moorlands which many farmers at the time were loath to plough, partly because it would limit the area available for hunting, the Exmoor farmers' only opportunity for a day off.

When Exmoor became a National Park many farmers could not see the point. Their land was privately owned; it did not belong to the nation and it was not a park, it was farmland; they feared restrictions on their way of life and work and an invasion of visitors crossing fields and leaving gates open.

The Park was set up with the aim of protecting the wild and remote landscape while paying due regard to the needs of farmers and foresters. No one envisaged any conflict and it was assumed by many that the farmer and forester managing the land would actually conserve the landscape. No one foresaw that developments in agricultural techniques and the pressure to produce more food and increase incomes would actually lead to damage and destruction of the protected landscape and to conflict between those who sought to conserve the moorland and those who needed to make the best economic use of their land.

During the sixties and seventies the government continued to encourage the farmer to produce as much food as possible. Many people gave up making hay and turned to silage, which could be made in almost any weather and was a more nourishing winter fodder than hay. Numbers of sheep and cattle increased and there were growing demands from farmers anxious to plough up moorland so that they might increase their stock. During the early sixties moorland was being lost to agriculture and afforestation at up to a thousand acres a year.

Round about the time that local government was being reorganised and a single National Park Committee set up (1974), some 'London folk' were beginning to question the effect that the government's agricultural policies were having on National Parks. On Exmoor the burning issue became that of moorland conversion and for a few years the loss of Exmoor's heather moorland made headline news.

It was a difficult time for all concerned. The farmers naturally looked to making the best economic use of

By 1951 horse and tractor were working side by side. Here the horse pulls the hay-rake. 'A wonderful machine' carries the hay up on to the wagon. Faster and far less effort than the pitchfork, it was one of many machines which were soon to make the farm labourer redundant.

their land encouraged by government grants. The Exmoor Society, a conservation pressure group, highlighted the potential loss of moorland, and spoke out passionately whenever possible. The National Park Committee, was caught in the cross-fire, faced with the task of finding a balance between the farming and conservation interest but without effective powers available for achieving this. There were no planning controls over ploughing up moorland or draining blanket bog.

Once the ructions had died down it was apparent that some useful consequences had emerged. As Ben Halliday pointed out in his speech at the Park's fortieth anniversary celebrations, 'Public attention had been drawn to one aspect of the much more widespread and complex problem of the impact that advancing agricultural technology was having on the countryside. This in turn fed everyone's growing preoccupation with the fragility of the countryside as a whole.

'At the local level, the Park Committee had, in fact, found a solution of a sort for its immediate problem of preserving the moorland and this, in turn, was to provide a pattern on which similar problems might be tackled in the broader national context.'

The solution had its origins in a pioneering management agreement with the owner of the Glenthorne Estate, concluded in 1979. This voluntary agreement included a measure of compensation for loss of potential income to the farmer who refrained from ploughing critical moorland. It was far from ideal, depending as it did on the co-operation of the farmer and protracted negotiation but nonetheless became a model for conservation agreements since. On Exmoor voluntary management agreements have resulted in the saving of over three thousand acres of moorland. The Porchester Report of 1977 was crucial in highlighting the importance of moorland and the survey and maps showing land that it was vital to protect are now something which every National Park has to produce.

Since the seventies' farming hey-day, there has been less emphasis on food production and many farmers have suffered a significant drop in income from husbandry. At the same time there has been increased pressure on them to manage their land in an environmentally friendly way. In January 1993, Exmoor was designated an Environmentally Sensitive Area (ESA).

This government scheme is designed to involve farmers in the protection of the traditional Exmoor landscape and in the provision of new opportunities for public access to enclosed farm land. Payments are available to help farmers manage all of their land in ways that benefit the environment by a range of measures. These include reducing grazing on heather moorland to promote the recovery of the vegetation, preventing the destruction of flower rich meadows by ploughing, drainage and the application of fertilisers and pesticides and the control of invasive bracken and rhododendrons. There are grants to help them repair traditional farm buildings and lay hedges, things which cost more in time and money but which are essential if the landscape is to be conserved. Although it is early days, signs are that this scheme is going to be a success and will benefit both farmers and Exmoor.

Market in the Auction Field at Exford c.1955.

The Incline on the West Somerset Mineral Railway, built to convey iron ore from the Brendon Hill mines to the port of Watchet.

Mining and Quarrying

There was mining for silver-lead at Combe Martin from the thirteenth century until 1875. Iron-mining on the Brendon Hills, as at Heasley Mill, Cornham and Wheal Eliza near Simonsbath, was sporadic and commercially short-lived. The first trial pits in the Brendon Hills were sunk in 1839 and in 1853 the Brendon Hills Iron Ore Company (later the Ebbw Vale Company) started commercial operations.

Fortunately perhaps for Exmoor, if not for the miners at the time, the high cost of extracting ore from the Brendon Hills and transporting it across to Wales together with competition from ore imported from Spain, soon made the venture uneconomic and the last pit finally closed in 1883. Later attempts to revive the industry were unsuccessful.

The village of Brendon Hill, which sprang up almost overnight, complete with church, chapel, shop and Miners' Literary Institute, has all but disappeared while the remains of the old West Somerset Mineral Line, built to convey the iron ore to Watchet, are grazed by sheep or shrouded in undergrowth. The area attracts many people including school groups, fascinated by what remains and eager to find out more.

The farmer at Burrow Farm has co-operated with the National Park Authority in allowing people to visit the ruined engine house while the Authority has been responsible for making the structure safe, setting up a marked footpath beside the old railway line and for providing information about the engine house and the mines.

Burrow Farm engine house c.1950. It housed the steam engine used to pump water out of the mines nearby.

The engine house after restoration.

Inside the cutting shed at Treborough Slate Quarry c.1900.

Spoil heap of slate off-cuts outside the cutting shed and stables c.1900.

View of the same area showing the spoil heap today.

There has been a blue slate quarry in Treborough Woods, owned by the Trevelyan family of Nettlecombe, since medieval times. In 1426, 2000 slate tiles were produced for Dunster Castle at a total of 20d but with carriage costing twice as much again. Many houses in the area are roofed or faced with slates and huge slabs form doorsteps, porch roofs and of course, tomb stones.The quarries were usually leased and had their ups and downs until 1938 when the land passed into other hands and working ceased for good. The tramlines and wagons went for scrap for the war effort and some buildings were pulled down. After the war the spoil heaps were planted with conifers while the biggest quarry across the road became a rubbish tip for the West Somerset District Council.

The quarries stand within ancient woodland and, thanks to a new owner, the stretch south of the road has been made into a nature reserve where the Exmoor Natural History Society has laid out a nature trail. The tip, which caused a major traffic problem in Roadwater, has now been closed, thanks to patient negotiation between National Park officers, Somerset County Council and the owner of the pit and the opening of a new landfill site near Williton.

Woodlands

Woodland has been evolving on Exmoor since the Ice Age and at one time the area was almost completely wooded. Over the last six thousand years or so, humans have gradually cleared the higher ground using the timber to build houses and fences, for fuel and to form utensils, implements, wheels and a myriad other things. Re-growth was prevented on the higher ground by the continuous grazing of ponies, sheep and cattle and by periodic burning.

Many of the broad-leaved woods that remain on Exmoor have survived because they went on being worked and valued for their products and as an additional source of income, well into this century. About a half of these woods are 'ancient woodland', at least four hundred years old and perhaps older. Amongst the gnarled branches, hung with curtains of lichen, you can smell the dank, damp, ancient scent of past centuries.

The most important commercial product in this century was tanbark. Many villages such as Alcombe, Porlock and Dulverton boasted a tannery where skins, from cattle, horses and sheep, were cured to make leather. The tannin was obtained from the bark

The tan bark shed at Porlock tannery c.1930.

of coppiced oaks. These trees are cut to the ground but dormant buds allow fresh young poles to grow which produce the highest levels of tannin preservative. Smallholders traditionally held an allotment of wood alongside their other land. In Hawkcombe Woods small strips of woodland were leased from the Blathwayt estate and worked on a twenty year rotation. Each year one strip of coppiced poles was ready for cutting and stripping the tanbark.

Charcoal burners are remembered in Culbone Woods and at Nutcombe Bottom, near Dunster and remains of charcoal burning can be found in many other woodlands. Charcoal was once the only fuel available which could produce the steady intense heat needed for iron-smelting and blacksmith work. It was used from the beginning of the Iron Age until the introduction of coke for smelting at the end of the eighteenth century.

All of these ways of working and managing woodland were gone by the sixties, leaving many woods without any form of management; old trees died and were not replaced while undergrowth thickened, stifling the ground flora below though providing good habitats for animals and insects. Government policy at this time was to encourage the planting of conifers as a fast-growing cash-crop. The unsuitability of large-scale planting of conifers on the open Exmoor landscape was brought home with the proposal in 1957 by the Forestry Commission and the Fortescue Estate to plant conifers on 1200 acres of open moorland on the Chains and Furzehill Common. The reasons for the proposal were not simply commercial. The Lynmouth flood disaster had occurred only five years earlier and it was hoped that planting the area

Porlock tannery workforce posed behind the tan-pits.

would slow down the run-off rate and help prevent such a thing happening again. The fear of losing this wild, wet area of moorland consolidated public opinion which encouraged the National Park Administration, then in its infancy, to resist the plans and eventually to win the day. A survey of woodland made soon after was well received nationally and set an example for other Parks to follow,

In 1977 the Porchester Report recognised that woodland, as well as moorland, was disappearing fast and this marked a turning point in attitudes to woodland on Exmoor. People began to recognise the significance of the diversity of habitat and wild life within the woods and that in ancient woodland like Horner Woods, now a Site of Special Scientific Interest, one can find evidence for a long history of woodland management and exploitation. Recently, archaeologists have discovered signs of occupation in Horner Woods dating back to the Iron Age. These woodlands also provide unique opportunities for ecological research since they contain so many scarce and vulnerable plants and animals.

At first the Park Authority protected threatened woodland by tree preservation orders, but in 1963 bought part of North Hill at Minehead after long negotiations to prevent felling, commercial afforestation and the denial of public access. This was the first of several purchases including part of Hawkcombe Woods and Birch Cleave at Simonsbath. The Park Authority now owns about 5% of Exmoor's principal woodlands.

The management of the Park Authority's ancient woods is traditional and labour intensive, the work being done by the Park estate staff. Special care is taken to maintain the beauty of the woodlands while at the same time opening up new tracks and paths and providing information so that more people may visit the woods and understand how they are being looked after. A new commercial venture that is proving successful is the production of barbecue style charcoal while the timber from woodland thinning is used by the estate staff to build bridges, stiles and fingerposts.

Working with horses in Hawkcombe Woods today.

Water

When, in the late 1820s, John Knight set two hundred Irish navvies to build a dam to enclose the head waters of the River Barle and form Pinkery Pond, he did not need planning permission and it is unlikely that anyone objected to what he was doing.

It was very different when, in the 1970s, the water authorities decided that it was essential for another reservoir to be built on Exmoor to supply water to local towns. Four sites were short-listed including Landacre, Bye Common with two in the Haddeo Valley. The National Park Committees were among many who resisted the idea but once the outcome became inevitable, assisted in choosing the site of least damage to the environment and ensuring that the new reservoir would blend with the landscape. A site in the Haddeo Valley was chosen.

South West Water retained Dame Sylvia Crowe to advise on the landscaping of the reservoir and the beauty of Wimbleball Lake, twenty years on, owes much to her meticulous and sympathetic planning. She wrote in the *Exmoor Review* (1975): 'The object throughout is to blend the reservoir and all its associated objects into the surrounding landscape so that it appears as a natural piece of water.' The concrete dam is a simple piece of engineering, carefully sited and built with local materials, aggregate from Holmingham's quarry at Cove and sand from Hillhead Quarry near Cullompton, to ensure a pinky tinge that blends with the local sandstones. 12, 000 trees and shrubs were planted to screen car parks and picnic areas and to disguise the hard rim of the reservoir.

From the first it was intended that Wimbleball should be a centre for quiet recreation, drawing people from some of the popular tourist 'honey pots' on Exmoor. Foot and bridlepaths were laid out by the National Park Authority and South West Water, while Somerset Trust for Nature Conservation turned 29 acres into a nature reserve. That Wimbleball Lake rarely appears crowded is largely due to Dame Sylvia's careful planning 'for the right number in the right place'.

The Haddeo Valley before building began at Wimbleball c.1975.

Wimbleball Lake today.

The Old Mill Horner

*Horner Mill restored
as a dwelling.*

Horner Mill c.1947.

Water wheels were once a familiar sight on Exmoor which used to be a region of small, local industries powered by the rivers and streams that rise on the moor. Most familiar are the mills for grinding corn but water power was also used in fulling cloth, sawing timber, operating forge hammers and sharpening blades. Some farms had their own water-wheel adapted for a range of purposes from grinding animal feed to crushing apples for cider-making. There were larger concerns as well like the foundry and the agricultural engineering works at Roadwater. In 1898 a hydro generating plant was installed at Lynmouth to provide the town's electricity. Others followed at Dulverton and Porlock. Although the Lynmouth generating station was destroyed in the 1952 flood disaster, electricity is still supplied to the National Grid by a new plant in the town.

A few mills survived the Second World War but most have been given up for far longer, the buildings deserted, the wheels allowed to rot and the once busy water leats silted up. Some corn mills have recently been restored. Dunster Mill and the mill at Combe Sydenham are now producing stone-ground flour on a commercial basis. Others have been turned into dwellings.

Fetching bread at Cutcombe during the 1947 winter.

Snow on Exmoor

'That night such a frost ensued as we had never dreamed of, neither read in ancient books, or histories of Frobisher. The kettle by the fire froze, and the crock upon the hearth-cheeks; many men were killed and cattle rigid in their head-ropes.'

R. D. Blackmore in *Lorna Doone*
(based on an eye-witness account of a
seventeenth century Exmoor winter).

'The terriblest winter this year ever since that one in 1776, that is 38 years ago. Began the 6th day of January, snow or three or four snows else, then a day's rain and froze to the ground, bushes, trees, hedges, broke them all down with the weight , which was two or three inches thick in some places of ice... Many sheep under snow, 29 Shortecombe and nine of them dead. Forced to take in every sheep from Shortecombe and give them hay.

'Forced to give hay to the Exmore colts and other colts. Go to mill on foot. No horse could go, the drifts were so high, forced to go over the fields, the roads mostly full, it were eight snows, it hold most five weeks.'

John Thorne
North Radworthy, 1814.

The winter of 1947

Once you could get out to take photographs, the worst was over. The snow reached over the hedges so that people standing on the drifts could touch the tops of the telegraph poles. As the cattle feed began to run out at Cloggs Farm, Hawkridge, Farmer Bawden seriously considered slaughtering his twenty cows by

Piles Mill, Allerford.

shooting them rather than letting them starve. 'Well,' said his wife, 'you'll have to shoot them two at a time since you've only got ten cartridges.' Fortunately for his Red Rubies, the relief lorry got through before this drastic action was necessary and his daughters remember their father throwing his hat in the air as the lorry was spotted, making its slow descent over the hill.

1947 is sometimes regarded as the last of the legendary Exmoor winters but in 1963 the snow was just as deep and lay on parts of the moor from Boxing Day until the beginning of May, while temperatures on average fell below those of 1947. 'The West Country blizzards, the marooned villages, the isolated farmsteads, the railway engines unable to complete their journeys, the abandoned cars, the sheep and ponies desperate for the essentials that retain life will be recalled a century hence,' wrote J. M. Slader in the

Exmoor Review later that year. The difference was that by 1963 there were 'helicopters and their crews striving to relieve the sick, feed the animals and supply daily bread. Snow was cleared from the roads by mechanical means. There was light and warmth at the turn of a switch and refrigerators and deep-freezes stocked to forestall the siege.'

The article concluded, 'Nature can no longer ruin a prosperous farm within a few months of severe winter weather.' While this may be true every Exmoor farmer knows there is never room for complacency as winter approaches.

Making a way through. This was a job that had to be done again and again as more snow fell and the wind blew the lying snow across the cleared paths.

Helicopter at Brushford in 1963. The welcome 'choppers' delivered hay, cattle cake, coal and diesel oil as well as provisions.

Rain

Heavy snow and great freezes on Exmoor are not unusual. Nor is heavy steady rain. The central Exmoor plateau, the gathering ground of dozens of small rivers, has a higher annual rainfall than most parts of Devon and Somerset and after storms, streams that are usually just shallow trickles can rapidly become rushing torrents.

The rains of the summer of 1952 were exceptional, falling onto the moorland, saturating the peaty soil till it was like a sponge that could hold no more. All through the summer the rivers rising on the Chains were just able to cope. Then came the storms of 15 August, 1952, when more than 9 inches (225mm) of rain fell on the Chains in 24 hours, turning every stream and rivulet into a torrent which poured off the moor in a raging flood. To the south the Barle uprooted trees, carried away the stones at Tarr Steps and flooded Simonsbath to a depth of ten feet. At Dulverton the river rose twenty feet above normal and there was widespread flooding at Exford.

To the north-west all the water poured into the narrow, steep-sided valleys of the East and West Lyn. The rushing rivers carried tree trunks, boulders and other debris in a remorseless flood towards the sea. In the narrow parts of the valleys and behind bridges the debris formed dams. Floodwater built up till they eventually burst and huge surges poured down the valleys. In the holiday town of Lynmouth, the arch of Lyndale Bridge could not take the flood and the river took a new course, sweeping away the tightly-packed houses and hotels that had been built on the flood plain. It was a night of fear and of heroism.

Norman and Violet Haynes kept Shelley's Cottage Hotel in Lynmouth and lived there with their sons, Richard and Gregory.

> I had laid the breakfast table for 27 guests, and then suggested to Norman that we walked down to see the river which I had been told was very high. Richard was playing with some of our guests, and Gregs was asleep in his cot in a downstairs bedroom. Our nearest neighbours, Barbara and Basil Ayres, had the greengrocery shop at the

Flood damage in Lynmouth.

Shelley's Cottage Hotel after the flood. Once the worst of the clearing up was done Violet and Norman Haynes were back in business.

crossroads. About ten people were sheltering there from the rain, and there seemed to be a steady trickle of water running into the shop. We helped move some of the stock upstairs out of the wet.

Then I looked up and saw a huge wall of water coming down Glen Lyn. I called out, 'Norman, I think that water will go over the wall - nobody knows Gregs is in the downstairs room. Norman ran out calling, 'I'll go and then come back for you.' Watching him, I saw him reach the telephone kiosk - the water struck it, and it toppled over. The water now swirled around me, waist deep; I hung on to the doorway, and as the wave hit me, the stone wall collapsed and I went down with it. I thought I was drowning... As I was rushed along, I managed to grasp the railings at the cross-roads. I pulled myself up and could feel the paving stones lifting under the force of the water. Others from the shop were now hanging on the railings, calling out, 'Get across to the Lyndale!' but I kept saying, 'I must get back to my children.' Then I heard Norman's voice, 'Vi! Vi! where are you?' I put out my hand into the inky blackness towards the sound... a warm hand grabbed mine, and he pulled himself up beside me. Some people were preparing to swim against the current to the Lyndale, but Norman and I, terrified for our children, linked arms and forced our way against the river, in the shelter of the chapel wall, up to the gate of Shelley's.

Our visitors were amazed at our condition. We told them to collect their belongings and put them in a room at the far side of the house. I went and got Gregs and wrapped him in a blanket. At that time the high garden wall was keeping the river back, but it was seeping underneath and the floor was spongy like wet blotting paper. Visitors brought us dry clothes while others looked after the children. One visitor gave me her own shoes and bound up a six inch cut in my leg. Two men went out to see what was happening; they came back saying, 'The river is building up - we must all leave!' At first Norman would not go but they persuaded him.

We walked up the Watersmeet Road, Norman carrying Gregs, Richard and I holding on to each other and to Norman's coat. The lightning was very bad and I was against going among the trees. Then Sid Berry came out of his cottage, saying, 'Come in here.' There were about thirty people sheltering in his two small rooms, mostly passing tourists. Gertie offered to dry my hair and I was horrified to see her snow white towel immediately covered with thick mud. My teeth too were gritting on mud. Their last candle was burning on the table. We knew that the worst time would be at high tide - sea against river - which would be about 2 a.m. Our candle died at 1.30 a.m. We were left in the darkness, with the roar of the river, rocks and houses tumbling, and screams for help. We could do nothing.

At daylight, I returned home for clothes for Gregs. On the way, I recognised items from Norman's workshop scattered along the path. I walked into the house, wading through thick mud. I looked through the lounge to the dining room, where there should have been an end wall. I could see right through to a racing river and Prospect Corner. In what was left of the room were huge boulders, tree trunks, overturned tables, bits of chairs ... and we were supposed to be expecting thirty new guests, next day...

Visitors started coming back. Norman found a Primus stove and we soon had a cup of tea going.

When the outside wall went, most of the bedroom furniture seemed to slide out; a few wet mattresses were lying about and some splintered pink wood I knew had been Gregs's cot. We started to move anything that looked reasonable to an upstairs room on the other side of the house. A guest who had been stopping in Room 12, came out, polishing his shoes. He complained about the noise that had gone on last night - he and his wife had been unable to sleep - he thought the other guests had had a wild party. I left somebody else to explain the circumstances!

The police evacuated the visitors first. Then it was our turn to climb into Lyndale, out to a balcony, down a ladder into the river (by now a lot lower), up another ladder to the half of Countisbury bridge still left. Then we climbed into a Black Maria and then later into a coach which took us to Minehead.

Mr C. H. Archer of Wootton Courtenay was one of several rain monitors working in Somerset in 1951, under the Somerset Rainfall Association whose work was later taken over by the River Boards. Mr Archer had set up rain gauges on Exmoor in order to make a special study of rainfall in the area and the morning after the flood set out to visit his gauges.

My round was a strenuous one. Owing to reported flooding in Exford I went via Winsford and thence along the hill-tops to the Exford-Simonsbath road, where I was met by a huge notice, 'Road Blocked', but I persevered. First obstruction was about level with Honeymead, where boulders and rubble had been piled up across the road, having been swept through a gateway on the northern slope. This feature recurred several times before Simonsbath.

Simonsbath was in a mess. The whole ground floor of the hotel had been swept clean by a sudden in-rush of flood-water in the small hours of the 16th. The surface of the main road was thoroughly disrupted mainly by flood-water bursting the surface open from underneath, both immediately below the hotel and 100 yards on at the

entrance to the Challacombe road. The roadway was completely swept away between these points and the bridge over the Barle, though the bridge itself still stood forlornly. It was utterly impossible for a car to reach the Barle bridge but with careful edging I was able to reach the Challacombe road. The first one-and-a-quarter miles of this road were very bad with constant holes.

After this preliminary summit, the road was somewhat less bad, but all bridges large or small from Honeymead onwards had balustrades and a good deal of surface swept away, and the road was constantly burst open from below, not only in the valleys where you might expect it, but on well drained hill-sides. In at least two cases that I noticed this was evidently due to the earth and stone walls which bound the fields in these parts having held the water till a minor reservoir was formed, when presently the weight of water punched a hole maybe 6ft. wide in the wall, and came up under the road surface at other points.

On the return journey I went via Exford, where the roads were clear of the floods but both hotels had squads of firemen, apparently engaged in pumping out flood-water. No damage east of Exford.

The mouth of the River Lyn before the flood.

The mouth of the River Lyn after the flood showing how the course of the river has been diverted and the river bed reinforced.

Living on Exmoor

Nearly all of the villages on Exmoor were in existence before they were recorded in Domesday Book, William the Conqueror's national tax return of 1086. While the names of many of the villages, Trentishoe, Selworthy, Timberscombe, Twitchen, show that they were firmly settled by the Saxons round about 800 AD, some may well have been older and many of the scattered farms that are not named in Domesday Book are just as ancient.

As we have seen, the Saxons abandoned the higher Exmoor plateau as a place to live (it was soon to become the Royal Forest) and chose more sheltered sites with a good water supply. Where the land was poorer the settlements were made up of scattered farmsteads with a church, perhaps built on an ancient holy site, and maybe a mill and a cluster of cottages nearby. A few villages grew to become market centres for the local farms and isolated hamlets, while on the coast, Combe Martin, Lynmouth and Porlock Weir developed as small fishing and trading ports.

By the end of the eighteenth century many Exmoor villages were in a depressed and dilapidated state. Even those which had become prosperous in the days of the Tudors and Stuarts like Dunster and Dulverton had seen a reversal in fortune, mainly as a result of the decline of the woollen industry. Yet by the third quarter of the nineteenth century most larger villages had become prosperous and near self-sufficient. This was due in part to landowners like John and Frederic Knight, Sir Thomas Dyke Acland and Mr Walter Halliday at Glenthorne who were turning their attention to improving their homes and estates and the living conditions of their tenants. This engendered jobs and put spending money into the

A cottage at Martinhoe. Before 1902.

The same cottage now Coronation Villa. After 1902.

pockets of farm tenants, craftsmen and shop-keepers, if not into those of the farm labourer. The Rev. Joseph Relph, coming from Cumberland to Exford in 1823 found a parish of scattered farms with no real village centre. His initiative, energy and inspiration led to improved roads linking with the centre of the Knight estates at Simonsbath, refurbished inns for travellers, new built cottages and workshops for craftsmen. Children went to dame schools and the poor were cared for. By 1851 the parish had a real centre and the population and number of houses had nearly doubled. Only the most isolated Exmoor churches escaped the hand of the Victorian restorer who in many places also built new rectories and schools.

More people were beginning to visit Exmoor, drawn there by the beauty of the scenery and this also contributed to a growing economy, at the same time bringing to the area a glimpse of other ways of living. Entrepreneurs built grand hotels to cater for the well-off visitor. Others decided to settle in the area, like Sir George Newnes, the founder of *Titbits*, who became the benefactor of Lynton and Lynmouth and was responsible for building Lynton Town Hall and the instigator of the Cliff Railway.

Parracombe showing the new church built in 1878, the Victorian vicarage and in the foreground, the Fox and Goose, formerly a coaching inn.

Exford before 1952 when the blacksmith's cottage (centre) was so badly damaged by the flood that it had to be pulled down.

A garage replaced the blacksmith's cottage at Exford.

The First World War saw the end of the old way of life in the villages. In every place, war memorials name the young men who did not return to inherit the great houses or the farms or to take their place in the haymaking teams. The depression in agriculture which followed meant that many families moved away from Exmoor altogether. It is no coincidence that the first school closures on Exmoor occurred in the late twenties and thirties as the number of children in the villages fell. Meanwhile other people moved to the area; wounded and shell-shocked soldiers seeking to restore their health, businessmen who had lost fortunes in the depression trying to eke out a meagre living along with artists and writers attracted by the colour and quiet of the moor.

Until the Second World War the people of Exmoor were still dependent on agriculture. After the war the links in the chain that bound them were gradually severed. Estates, no longer viable, were broken up and farms sold. As heavy horses were replaced by tractors and skilled farm labourers by machinery, fewer and fewer people were needed to work on the land. Young people had to look elsewhere for work and, with jobs scarce around Exmoor, many again had to move away. Others responded to the challenge by adopting new ways of work and stayed to make a success of them.

Some of those who wanted to stay found it impossible to afford houses since properties, made vacant by farm workers, were being snapped up by buyers from towns with plenty of money who wanted second or retirement homes or to start a new life in the country. Prices soared out of reach of local people. This trend is continuing as farms bought from estates after the war are being sold on. Sometimes the bulk of the land is sold to a neighbouring farm to make a viable unit and just the farmhouse and a few acres retained as a private house.

People buying second homes do not often get involved in the life of the community although those moving in permanently do, and sometimes attempt to take over, trying to run things in what they consider to be a more efficient way! They do not always realise that they are newcomers to a community that has been established for centuries or that they have come to live in the country, not in the suburbs. Criticism of tractors holding up traffic does not go down well; joining in and helping to keep things going is valued.

Tourism has provided a great boost to the local economy and can help to maintain village services - post office, shop, garage, pub - which might otherwise be forced to close. If a village is on the right route or suitably attractive then it is likely to survive, unless, of course, it is overwhelmed by cars, visitors and tea shops. Others are in a gentle decline.

The Park Authority tries to help communities play their part in looking after Exmoor by supporting projects which are in accord with their obligations and which, at the same time, help to promote the social and economic well-being of the community. Examples are the Exmoor Community Bus which carries both tourists and local passengers and the establishment of Park Information Agencies in some village shops to encourage trade. Recently the Park Authority has been involved in the setting up of the Exmoor Producers' Group which is working to raise the profile of Exmoor produced goods.

Nettlecombe Court and deer park c.1900, family home and estate of the Trevelyan family for more than 500 years.

Nettlecombe Court is now run as a centre by the Field Studies Council for the Leonard Wills Trust. Like many of the big estates on Exmoor, the Nettlecombe Estate has been broken up and the farms sold away, mostly to their previous tenants. Many of the big houses are no longer occupied by families. Dunster Castle belongs to the National Trust while Holnicote House is owned by the Holiday Fellowship. Large tracts of land on Exmoor are now owned by organisations like the Badgworthy Land Company, the National Trust and of course, the National Park itself.

The Village School

The school is often the indicator of a lively and active community though with present day education policies preferring larger primary schools, there are several sizeable villages in the Park, equally lively and active, but whose children are bussed to school elsewhere. Schools began to be closed on Exmoor between the wars as pupil numbers dropped. Hawkridge was closed for a short while during the Second World War, its pupils walking to Withypool. The school at Oare remained open until there were only two pupils, one the headmistress's daughter. Wootton Courtenay school closed in 1946. Recently other schools have closed, some quite sizeable, in spite of strong resistance from their communities which saw school closure as yet another nail in the coffin of community life. Many old school buildings have been turned into dwellings, though at Allerford the school is now a Museum and children dress up to occupy the desks of the Victorian schoolroom.

Now the village school acts as a focus for the scattered community in the area, often holding classes and social events as well as being a day-to-day meeting point for parents as well as children. The shop and garage in the village with the school may also benefit.

Allerford school is now the West Somerset Rural Life Museum. Part of their service for schools includes a lesson Victorian-style in the restored school-room.

Allerford school before its closure in 1981.

Martinhoe National School 1897.

The Village Shop

In Timberscombe in 1935 there was a butcher, a post office, two general shops, a shoe dealer and a grocer to serve a scattered farming community of nearly 400 people. Today the population is about the same and new houses are being built but the last shop has recently closed although the post office survives. The demise of the village shop is commonplace today throughout the country, the result of a combination of circumstances ranging from greater mobility and the development of the supermarket to the use of freezers and the emergence of shopping as a recreational activity rather than a necessity.

In an area like Exmoor where many people live a long way from large shopping centres and where there is little, if any, public transport, the village shop still provides for day-to-day needs and for the elderly and those without a vehicle. However this custom is rarely enough to keep the business going. In some places the village shop and post office is hanging on by the skin of its teeth relying on the tourist trade to give it enough of a boost in summer to keep it going for the dwindling local trade in winter. At Wootton Courtenay the shop has become a co-operative owned by shareholders in the village while in several places including Brompton Regis, Challacombe, Wheddon Cross and Withypool, the Park Authority has set up Information Agencies in the village shops which help to draw visitors.

Between the wars and for a short while afterwards, there were numerous travelling shops. People living in small villages and on isolated farms are still glad of deliveries.

Allerford village shop and post office.

David Pile, general builder 1994.

Mr Huxtable, mason and carpenter c.1900.

The Newton family were masons, carpenters, blacksmiths and wheelwrights. The wheelwright business at West Knowle, near Dulverton c.1900.

Until the end of the nineteenth century practically every job on Exmoor was linked with the land or with the people who worked on the land. Each person was skilled at a particular craft or task. The shepherd, carter, ploughboy; the mason, tiler, joiner; the wheelwright and the blacksmith; the tailor, the cobbler and the straw bonnet maker; the parlourmaid, the baker and the inn keeper. The list seems endless.

Now nearly every job has either disappeared or been transformed by developments in technology. The wheelwright's shop has become a motor garage while the combine harvester does the work of ten in a quarter of the time. At first these changes drove people to look for work elsewhere but gradually fresh openings have emerged. Providing for tourists is now the main source of employment on Exmoor while

many people, rather like the old specialist craftsman, have started their own businesses in response to new needs, often working from home.

A tailoring business at Cutcombe about 1920. From left to right: Mr Spiller, Robert Melhuish sen., Charlie Western, George Carter, Robert Melhuish jun., Ernest Hoyles, Alfred Vaulter.

This business at Dulverton provides high-tech services for many other home-based enterprises.

Simonsbath

Simonsbath was originally just the name given to a place where several rough tracks converged to cross over the River Barle. Situated at the heart of the old Royal Forest, there was no house there until, in 1654, what is now the Simonsbath House Hotel was built for James Boevey, owner of the Forest during the Commonwealth period. It remained the sole habitation until the Forest was sold to John Knight in 1818. He, and later his son, managed the estate from Simonsbath and although his own house was never completed, farm buildings and cottages, church, parsonage, school and inn soon made up a nucleated village. An awareness of the history of the area and the interest of visitors led to the Refreshment House being named after William Rufus, the Norman king particularly interested in hunting, who was killed in the New Forest in 1100.

After the Fortescues bought the Exmoor estates, Simonsbath continued to be the centre of working operations. More houses were built and the population grew. In the early 1950s Simonsbath was still a busy farming community with school, shop, post office and a parish priest of its own. Gradually these all disappeared but after a short period in the doldrums Simonsbath has emerged as a vital centre for tourism. It is a natural starting point for exploring Exmoor on foot and its neglected buildings have been restored to provide for the needs of the passing visitor. The Park Authority has provided a car park, toilets and a lovely picnic area by the river while the beech woods which they own nearby at Birch Cleave are a beautiful and peaceful place to walk.

Simonsbath c.1994.

Simonsbath c.1900.

Dunster

Dunster High Street in 1954, the year that the Dunster Castle Estates were put up for sale.

Dunster Castle and its surrounding estates were owned by just two families, the de Mohuns and the Luttrells, from the time of William the Conqueror. The open High Street was used as a market place even before 1253 when Reginald de Mohun granted the burgesses of Dunster the right to hold a weekly market. A thriving woollen industry developed and in about 1609 the octagonal Yarn Market was built for the sale of cloth. The industry declined in the late eighteenth century and many people moved away leaving houses standing empty but, with the help of the Luttrells, the coming of the railway and various building projects, the village began to recover and by the end of the Victorian period was popular with visitors and with people retiring to the area. Several new houses were built on the edge of the village during the Victorian period but ownership by the Luttrells, of most of the land and property, prevented inappropriate development.

Now Dunster is geared to tourism. So many people come that they are in danger of spoiling what they have come to see. Car parks fill quickly in summer and vehicles are then parked in every available space. People need refreshments and enjoy souvenir shopping and some only see the crowded High Street lined with gift and tea shops. Many visit the castle and its gardens, now owned by the National Trust, but far fewer people discover the quieter church, village gardens, tithe barn, mill and packhorse bridge. The National Park Authority is concerned to maintain a balance in Dunster so that the essence of the place is not lost nor overwhelmed by crowds and cars while at the same time having in mind the needs of the people of Dunster who make their living by providing for visitors.

Dunster High Street, 1994.

Porlock Weir and Combe Martin

Unloading coal at Porlock Weir. The last cargo of coal was brought in on the Democrat *in 1950.*

Combe Martin, working harbour. Iron ore, silver and lead were shipped from Combe Martin during the nineteenth century while limestone and culm were imported for burning in the town's eighteen kilns. Much of the lime was used on John Knight's Exmoor estate. Combe Martin was famous for its strawberries during the 1920s.

Combe Martin, holiday resort. By the 1950s the town was growing in popularity as a seaside resort.

Thatcher at work at Selworthy Green c.1920.

Building on Exmoor

Traditionally Exmoor farmhouses and cottages were built with walls of local red sandstone or cob, and roofed with thatch, slate or tiles from Bridgwater or Minehead. In most villages buildings like this rub shoulders with others put up by the Victorians or in the thirties. Since Exmoor became a National Park the Authority has done its best to encourage new building which is in sympathy with its surroundings.

The planning powers of the Park Authority are little different from those of other local authorities so, unless a building is listed, it has no control over small 'improvements' which sometimes would be more suitable in suburbia than on Exmoor. Clean cut lines and sharp angles feel wrong in the country where nature's lines are curved and irregular. Natural building materials and traditional windows are often thought expensive and may require more maintenance but do blend with the surroundings. Some

These houses at Stoney Street, Luccombe, built in 1992 for the West Somerset Rural Housing Association on National Trust land, are an example of how new building can blend with its surroundings without being dull. They were awarded a Civic Trust commendation for their contribution to the quality and appearance of the environment.

people feel that tighter planning controls are needed to avoid both destroying traditional buildings and spoiling them by inappropriate treatment as well as ensuring that new buildings fit in well.

In 1958 the Park Administration published, 'Building on Exmoor', the first guide to good design for new building in National Parks and regarded as a model for other authorities. A second guide followed in 1977. A new 'Exmoor Design Guide' is being published in 1994.

Johnnie Jones delivering the mail to Mrs Reed at Red Deer Farm between Simonsbath and Exford before the First World War.

Roger delivering the mail to Mr and Mrs Bickersteth at Gallon House (formerly Red Deer Farm) May, 1994.

Above: *Nearly everyone in the parish gathered to celebrate the centenary of the dedication of St Luke's Church, Simonsbath in 1956.* Below: *The congregation, gathered from parishes in the united benefice of Exford, Simonsbath, Withypool and Hawkridge, after morning service at St Luke's Simonsbath in May 1994.*

The Farming Community

I think that if I tried to talk about something called 'community' with an Exmoor farmer, I would probably be looked at askance. Better words could be friendship, kinship, mutual understanding, comradeship but what it all boils down to is that wherever Exmoor people are, they are moulded by the same land, the same weather, the same hardship and the same pleasures. They understand what their neighbours are going through and they understand what makes them tick.

This sense of what outsiders call community is deep-rooted and isn't limited by parish boundaries. Sharing experiences, working together, attending funerals, the Exmoor farmer looks to his neighbour and shares the good and bad times. He takes hunting for granted - arguments about hunting nearly all stem from incomers and townsfolk who are so much further from the land and its wildlife than those who struggle to make their living from it. That the Exmoor National Park Authority, in spite of accusations over the years of interference has, in the tiny timespan of forty years, managed to establish itself alongside the farming community is no mean feat, when people who have moved into the area are still thought of as incomers after more than a generation.

The Exmoor village can never be the same as its lowland counterparts. With parishioners so many miles away, situated down a couple of miles of rough track and working all hours, there can be no casual coffee mornings. At Brompton Regis Women's

Meet of the Dulverton West Foxhounds at Cloggs Farm, Hawkridge 1993.

Institute, refreshments are a two course supper prepared by members in turn. 'We are working on the farm up to the last moment. We come straight to the meeting from the milking and by the end we are hungry!' Very different from the tea and biscuits that are all that their lowland neighbours need.

The community centres still around the sacred and the secular, the church and the village hall. Although farmers and their families find it hard to attend regularly the basic tenets and practice of the church seem still to underlie their way of life.

The village hall, often a memorial to those killed in the First World War, represents the secular. It is the setting for wedding receptions and eightieth birthday parties as well as flower shows, whist drives, Christmas dances, play groups and parish meetings. That so much money has been raised recently to build new halls at Monksilver and Brushford and improve those at Brompton Regis and Skilgate is an indication of just how thriving the Exmoor communities still are.

Anstey Flower Show 1990.

Meet in North Molton town square c.1910.

Ponies - a community concern

Have you ever considered just what the Exmoor Pony and the Giant Panda have in common? They are, in fact, both extremely rare and perhaps the most surprising thing is that there are fewer pure-bred Exmoor Ponies in the world than there are Pandas. At the last count in 1991 there were fewer than 800 pure-bred ponies and more than 1200 pandas and of the 800 ponies, only 300 were breeding mares.

The Exmoor Pony is unique. It has lived on the moor longer than humans have and is almost certainly the direct descendant of the prehistoric horse. Through living out on the open moor in all weathers the Exmoor has developed a real hardiness, with a special two-layer protective winter coat that repels the rain in winter and allows the snow to sit on its back without melting. Cross-breeding can detract from this hardiness making the pony less able to cope with winter conditions. It is wild inasmuch as it lives freely on open moorland all the year round, but every pony on Exmoor has an owner and belongs to one of eight herds, each with its own territory.

Until the advent of the tractor and motor car, the Exmoor Pony was a working animal, carrying the farmer to oversee his sheep and to market and his children to school; pulling carts, traps and sleds and sometimes being used to draw the plough and haul

Exmoor ponies on Holden Hill above Wilsham c.1954.

timber. Some were sold away as trustworthy children's ponies or to work underground in the coal pits. The changes in transport and in the pits lessened demand and so fewer ponies were bred. Then during the war horrific incidents led to a catastrophic decline in the numbers of ponies. Criminal butchers came at night, drove ponies living free on the moor into narrow lanes and stole them away to be slaughtered for meat. Others are said to have been killed by soldiers practising on the moor who used them for target practice. A further problem was that, with the coming of the motor car, gates onto the moor were constantly left open, ponies strayed and so some farmers decided it was better to keep them in fields near the farms than on the open moor.

By the end of the war there were only 50 pure-bred free-living Exmoor Ponies left. Only the hard and dedicated work of individuals like Mary Etherington, the daughter of the Rector of Withypool, the scientist, James Speed and members of the Exmoor Pony Society saved the breed and at last numbers are increasing.

Present day problems include concerns with the limited number of breeding strains and a fear that the hardiness of the pony may be lost through the apparently caring action of owners worming the animals and feeding hay in winter. If the pony is to stay true to type it needs to cope with these problems on its own.

In 1980 there was still great concern about the future of the Exmoor Pony and so the National Park Authority, anxious to commit itself to the conservation of the Exmoor Pony, decided to buy young stock and establish two new herds which they would own and look after themselves.

One of the new herds now runs free on Exmoor Forest, the ancient home of the ponies until they were ousted by more and more sheep in the last century. The other has its home on Haddon Hill just above Wimbleball Reservoir where the sight of the ponies gives delight to the many walkers and riders that visit the area.

It is not just ponies that are rare but certain birds, insects, and plants like this Club Moss.

78

Overhead wires at Porlock. Now you see them! Now you don't!
The Exmoor National Park Authority worked hard and long to get rid of these wires.

Travelling Over Exmoor

Dicky Slader, pedlar, poet, hymn-writer and one of the last Exmoor eccentrics, with his donkey, Eva Mini Mona Francis Adelaide Hamilton Jesse. He lived at Molland Cross between South Molton and Yarde Down and died in 1926 leaving behind a fund of stories that have been absorbed into Exmoor folklore. He used to walk long distances with his donkey to sell his wares - to Lynton, Ilfracombe, Barnstaple and Bideford. It was common up until the Second World War for people to walk 15 to 20 miles to sell their goods at pannier markets or shows and then walk back at the end of the day.

Walking for pleasure at Bossington.

Dicky Slader, the pedlar poet.

This century has seen tremendous changes in the way that people get about. Up until the 1940s children were still walking several miles to school in all weathers relying on the huge tortoise stoves to dry themselves and their clothes in wet weather (in the winter anyway). Some people walked to work, six or more miles there and back, and one woman from the the now deserted village of Clicket, near Timberscombe, is remembered for having walked to her work in Porlock each day, a round trip of 15 miles.

Although a few families were beginning to acquire motor cars by the thirties, most farmers continued to travel to market on horseback while their wives visited the local village shop by pony and trap. Petrol rationing during the Second World War meant that these practices continued well into the fifties. There were few occasions to travel much further afield and for many people, the 'tother side of Taunton' was a long way off.

Farmer Bawden ready to leave for market.

Wagon outside Cutcombe School c.1910. Extra horses have been hitched on to help the load up the hill from Timberscombe.

The pony and trap continued to be used by many people on the moor until after the Second World War.

The Minehead-Dulverton stage-coach outside the Carnarvon Arms, Brushford c.1900.

Right up until the 1920s the mail coach continued to be the main form of public transport over the moor itself. The stage coach linked Minehead with Lynmouth and Dulverton. A few years ago Mrs Rosamond Fisher recalled how as children she and her brothers and sisters were taken every year by coach to Lynton as a treat.'Once, just before Culbone Stables, where the horses were changed, we came into a complete blockage of the road by (early) motor cars following the hounds. George Folly (the driver) was furious. "The coach is a Royal mail. You can't hold us up!" He handed the reins to me and went to look for "The Lord" - he'd soon get them moving! "The Lord" was Lord Fortescue who indeed did clear the route.' In the winter a double-horse bus took the place of the coach two or three times a week while horse brakes visited some of Exmoor's beauty spots during the season.The Lorna Doone coach has survived and is now used occasionally as a tourist attraction.

By the middle of the First World War, motor buses were beginning to replace the coach and to provide services on other routes. The famous Blue Motors which travelled between Minehead, Porlock and Porlock Weir began running in 1916 while the Red Deer motor coaches provided four return trips every day save Sunday, between Exford and Minehead, each journey taking an hour and a quarter. The Royal Blue long distance motor coach crossed Exmoor providing a direct link between Dulverton, Minehead and Taunton. By the late twenties most villages were served by buses. As a 1926 Guide to Minehead said,'The picturesque four-in-hand coaches have now given way to the ubiquitous motor coach' and run occasionally in the summer to places of interest. The old waggonette that used to carry church choirs and Sunday schools on village outings was replaced by the charabanc and trips to Weston-super-Mare and Ilfracombe replaced picnics at very local beauty spots.

Blackmoor Gate railway station c.1930.

At the beginning of the twentieth century, railway lines surrounded Exmoor and many people were within easy reach of a station. Some travelled daily by train to schools and offices while others made a weekly journey on market days. There were even through trains from Paddington to Minehead and to Dulverton although a journey from Barnstaple to Chard and back took all day and involved five changes.

Goods traffic was equally important. In the parcel van milk churns, newspapers and the mail rubbed shoulders with boxes of day-old chicks, baskets of racing pigeons, cream and hampers of delicacies from Barkers in Kensington High Street. Cattle and sheep driven off the moor, were carried in cattle trucks to the London markets while, in the fifties, pre-myxomatosis, rabbits destined for up-country tables travelled on the special 'rabbit train'. Horse boxes with accommodation for grooms were sometimes attached to passenger trains. Coal and bulk fertiliser were brought to the stations and stored before delivery by lorry out to the farms.

The railway also brought the visitors.

Great numbers of people visited Exmoor for their holidays during the thirties and just after the war. Several people have told me that they think there were just as many visitors then as now. Some came by car but most by train, taking a bus on to the hotel, guest house or private accommodation where they would stay for a week or a fortnight. They would go out each day, perhaps walking or riding, but very often taking the bus to one of the popular beauty spots: Dunster, Lynmouth, Tarr Steps, Horner Woods, returning late in the day for an evening meal.

Stan Curtis remembers hot summer days in the mid thirties when, as a lad of six or seven, he stayed at Badgworthy Cottage with his great-uncle Jack Jones, shepherd on the Badgworthy herding. Stan recalls the 'flocks' of walkers streaming up from Malmsmead to see the famous Doone Valley and buying glasses of Eiffel Tower lemonade which he mixed from crystals and sold to the visitors at 6d a tot.

At Luccombe, visitors came back regularly, year after year, to stay in the same cottage. There was no formal advertising of accommodation, landladies depending on personal recommendation and word of mouth to fill their rooms. Most countrywomen treated their visitors as friends, welcoming this contact with the outside world. Holidays were fun if the visitors' books, kept for years, are anything to go by.

> If you stay with Mrs Tame
> You are sure to come again
> For she lives just down the lane
>   Does Mrs Tame

> Never were the rooms so clean
> While her cooking is a dream
> And she lives just by the stream
>   Does Mrs Tame

> When you come back tired and hot
> Tea is ready like a shot
> For she's always on the spot
>   Is Mrs Tame

> Should you crave for worms or string
> Books, pills, any mortal thing!
> You have only got to ring
>   For Mrs Tame.

> There's no trouble she won't take
> A nice holiday to make
> Have you tried the currant cake
>   Of Mrs Tame?

> So you'd better book your room
> And you'd better do it soon
> For she lives in Lucky Combe
>   Does Mrs Tame.
>
>   Luccombe 1931
>   *Exmoor Village*

Messrs Arnold and Hancock, the Wiveliscombe Brewers, owned twenty-five licensed houses on the moor in the early fifties, ranging from the Crown at Exford to the Poltimore Arms at Yarde Down. In evidence given at the National Park Inquiry in 1954 their representative said, 'Generally speaking the visitors to Exmoor are professional and business people who find in the solitude that Exmoor provides that relaxation that they require for their mental and

Motor cars at Winsford 1910.

physical well-being. Our Residential Hotels in their brochures offer such attractions as fishing, riding, visits to historical places, literary associations and botanical excursions, and the study of birds and wild animals.'

Another visitor came from London and stayed with Mrs Tame in Luccombe during October 1942, at the height of the blitz. She wrote of her visit, 'In these troubled times it has been possible to find peace, perfect peace for a few days at Porch Cottage, thanks to the excellent attention of Mr and Mrs Tame. God willing, I shall return to this haven of rest to take full advantage of all the good things to be found here.' The National Park Authority continues to encourage the quiet enjoyment of Exmoor.

Malmsmead c.1900.

Malmsmead, April 1994. The farm is now a shop and café. Hedges have been removed from the fields to allow access for machinery but trees and bushes, no longer needed for firewood, have been allowed to grow up around the bridge.

At Malmsmead.

We reached the farm at twilight. While our evening meal was preparing I had time to run out and stand on the bridge to watch the trout poised in the clear water below. Day and night the sound of the river was audible in John Ridd's farm.

The first evening meal I have never forgotten. A deep dish of Devonshire cream, and a loaf of brown bread and lightly boiled fresh eggs, were set before us on a lamp-lit, tea-laid table in a room smelling of the peat fire glowing red on the open hearth; indeed the smell of burning peat permeated the whole room - the curtains smelt of it, the Devonshire cream tasted of it!

Llewellyn Powys
Somerset Essays, 1937

88

Picnicking near Luccombe c.1950.

A walking party c.1938.

Looking north-west over Lynton from a spot near Summerhouse Hill c.1950.

When Exmoor became a National Park in 1954, there were no fears of the moor being over-run with visitors. Indeed, one of its advantages was that 'it would certainly attract holiday visitors from all parts of the country' and Lynton and Lynmouth Urban District Council, for example, supported the move to make Exmoor a National Park just because it would encourage more visitors to come to the area. They would travel to Exmoor by train or motor coach and be mainly 'walkers, cyclists, riders and campers and students of nature.' Of course a certain number of motorists were anticipated as well but with Exmoor about two hours drive from the nearest conurbations, they were expected to be few and far between.

The coming of the family motor car altered the pattern of visitor behaviour on Exmoor. Now lots of people wanted to drive over the moor, stop to look at the view and perhaps go for a walk. At first the poor roads discouraged motorists but minor roads out on the moor had been improved as part of the preventive measures package after the Lynmouth floods in 1952. As people became more affluent and had more holidays there were soon too many cars on the roads for comfort and people needed places to park. The Park Authority made small off-road parking areas near view-points and these were followed with landscaped car parks at honey-pot sites.

It was thought that the motorway would mean yet more cars for Exmoor, people from say, Birmingham, being able to come to Exmoor for the day. In fact with both the motorway and the more recent North Devon Link Road there has been a tendency for people to ignore Exmoor and go shooting past to Devon and Cornwall. Although there seem to be fewer cars and

Cars parked just off the road at Rex Stile Head, Dunkery looking towards Dunster c.1955. Lay-bys have been made at view-points like this to prevent indiscriminate parking and erosion.

coaches about than there were in the sixties, the number of vehicles travelling the narrow Exmoor roads is still a problem, not just practically but because the volume of traffic actually detracts from the wild and remote nature of the moor. A recent survey by the Countryside Commission has put Exmoor among the ten places in the country most threatened by the motor car.

Park and ride schemes have been tried on Exmoor. They started well but then began to fizzle out, motorists seeming to prefer the freedom of their own vehicles. Recently, however, there has been less opposition to leaving the car, and bus schemes are being revived with, initially, a good reponse. In the end people have to decide for themselves that too many cars are spoiling their enjoyment and then use some other means of visiting the area.

Outside the Nunnery, Dunster c.1950.

Outside the Nunnery, Dunster c.1974. The volume of traffic through Dunster is still tremendous but at least the flow is now regulated by traffic lights.

When John Eustace Anderson visited Minehead for a month's holiday in 1899, he and his companions got lost in Selworthy Woods. In his journal he describes how they visited Selworthy Green where they ordered tea at Mrs Rawle's before ascending to the church where a 'cheery old lady' showed them round. They then set out to walk to Bossington. 'They said it was easy to find the right path. Instead of that we lost our way... At last, after wandering about in all directions, we got down to a high five-barred gate, which the ladies had to climb somehow or other, and not having been country girls, they found it a little difficult. We then found ourselves near a farmhouse, as it was getting dusk, 6.40 p.m. Here, fortunately, by the merest chance, we stumbled across our man with the landau, who did not know what had become of us. I was very anxious as one of our ladies was not strong and could not walk far.

The losing ourselves quite spoilt the pleasure of the afternoon. I thought a few direction posts would have been of great use, but then they spoil the rusticity of the scene. No more wandering in an unknown wood for me if I can help it.'

One of the main things that the Park Authority tries to do is to help people enjoy the peace and beauty of Exmoor. Although there are plenty of experienced walkers who visit Exmoor there are also many people who are not 'country girls' and who can be quite anxious about leaving their cars and the familiar tarmac and setting out for a walk.

When in 1963, the Park Administration first appointed rangers, known then as wardens, the Somerset warden, Jim Collins, was particularly interested in making it possible for everyone to walk and ride on Exmoor without anxiety even if they could not read a map. Of the 700 miles of rights-of-way in the National Park at that time, only a very small percentage was signposted and free of obstruction. Footpath clearance and signposting began at once and has continued ever since. In order to develop more satisfying walks the wardens entered into negotiations with farmers and landowners who gave permission for people to walk over their land without giving up their rights. A method of 'way-marking' paths with different coloured paint was developed to make it easy for people to find their way. Both pioneering schemes and the way-marked walks guides won wide acclaim and the latter became an exemplar for walks literature throughout the country. John Eustace Anderson would have approved!

The Somerset warden, Jim Collins, putting the finishing touches to a direction post on the newly opened coast path on North Hill, 1975.

One of the most important aspects of the Park Authority work is helping members of the public enjoy their visit to Exmoor as much as possible. For some people, the whole concept of a National Park is something new and strange. A sign outside Minehead proclaims, 'Minehead. The Gateway to the National Park', and it is not unusual to come across people searching for an actual gate leading to a park of the kind with which they are familiar. Helping people to understand what a National Park is and what it is trying to achieve is a crucial part of the Authority's work, especially these days when countryside everywhere is under threat and the lessons of the National Park apply universally.

The first Visitor Centre where people could go for information was established at Minehead in 1963 followed by Centres at Combe Martin (1967), Lynmouth and Dulverton (1975), County Gate (1978) and Dunster (1983). At first a temporary caravan was used as a summer information centre at County Gate, 1000' up on the coastal road between Porlock and Lynmouth. It worked well for the first couple of years but then it was decided to re-site it and get it set up well in advance before the season began. That night a great gale blew up and the next morning the caravan was matchwood and the leaflets scattered to the four winds. It proved a salutary lesson reminding the National Park staff that in the end, it is always Exmoor that is in control.

More than four and a half million visitors have passed through the Centres since they were first set up and the staff have dealt with countless telephone and written enquiries. There are sometimes some interesting questions! 'Is that big hill still at Porlock?' 'I went to Longleat yesterday and a monkey bit me. Do your monkeys bite?' 'I'm thinking of getting a divorce. Can you advise me, please?' And, 'Can you read the map for me, please. I can't read it because I've got my hat on!' All questions are answered seriously!

In 1985 a free newspaper, the *Exmoor Visitor*, was launched which has proved extremely popular. It carries advertising for accommodation and attractions as well as basic information about the Park and how to make the most of a visit. It is reckoned that about two thirds of all visitors to Exmoor see the newspaper, many taking it home as a souvenir and to plan for next year's visit. Work began on the first handbook to Exmoor National Park in 1959 and since then a vast range of publications from information leaflets and guides to scholarly books on specialist subjects has been produced.

Every year thousands of young people visit Exmoor, some on Duke of Edinburgh Award Expeditions, or write to Exmoor House seeking information for

Exmoor National Park Authority battles with the elements ... and loses!

Pinkery Farm in 1970 just after it was bought as part of the Pinkery Estate by Somerset County Council. It was leased by the National Park Committee to the Education Department as a centre for outdoor education. In 1994 the buildings were taken back by the Park Authority to run as its own centre.

school projects. Exmoor Park Authority was one of the first Parks to employ a Youth and Schools Liaison Officer in 1975 and since then has developed a wide range of educational services which includes giving talks to local schools, accompanying visiting groups, preparing support materials and answering specialist enquiries from A level and degree students. Some groups of young people have been involved in regular volunteer work helping the rangers with various conservation tasks like clearing rhododendrons on moorland, where they are rapidly becoming a pest, or picking up litter, never a popular job!

Rangers are often asked, 'Where do you look after the animals?' Children, particularly, think that a ranger's job must be like that of Ranger Smith in the Yogi Bear films who looks after Yogi Bear and Booboo in Jellystone Park. Rangers on Exmoor don't 'look after' animals. They are the people who are out and about

meeting the public, keeping an eye on the area of the Park for which they are responsible. It is sometimes said that their 'bit of the business' is to be the eyes and ears of the National Park Officer.

When it comes to protecting wildlife it is the conservation of habitat - the moorland, the woodland, the seashore - that is so important. And often it is tiny areas where special conditions prevail - just the right altitude, dampness, temperature, plants for food - that have combined over the years to make those places exactly right for particular, and often rare, species like the heath fritillary butterfly, club moss, the otter and the dormouse, the cirl bunting, the merlin and the peregrine falcon. As the Park Authority works to protect the landscape it is protecting habitats at the same time and encouraging the increase of endangered species which might otherwise become extinct.

Ranger Mike Leach gives directions.

What of the Future?

Sometimes people ask, 'What would Exmoor be like today if it had not become a National Park in 1954?' It is, of course, an impossible question to answer but some things seem certain.

First and foremost, when Exmoor became a National Park it made people aware of the importance of its landscape. If it had not been made a National Park, a great deal more open moorland would have been lost to the plough or to afforestation than the 12, 000 acres that we know have disappeared since 1947. This greater loss of moorland would have been accompanied by the dilution of those elements which make Exmoor so special; its varied landscapes, its openness and sense of freedom, its air of remoteness and of not being tampered with. The improved and cultivated land would have had to be fenced so access for walking and riding would have been restricted and with more and more land converted to similar use, distinctive and scarce habitats would have disappeared, reducing the variety of Exmoor's wildlife.

Other alterations to the face of Exmoor have taken place more subtly through the abandonment of traditional management of both farmland and woodland, largely for economic reasons. This could have been even more damaging without the vigilance of the Park Authority which sets an example by working its own land in traditional and restorative ways as well as offering support to the farmer who is willing to do the same.

Working out ways to protect moorland did not happen overnight and it has taken the best part of forty years for the Park Authority to establish good working relationships with the Exmoor farmer who, to quote Ben Halliday, now views the National Park Officer 'more like a friend in high places who has helped to provide a lifeline against the inevitable reform of the Common Agricultural Policy.'

Besides moorland, Exmoor has some of the most beautiful coastline in Britain. A glance at neighbouring areas shows how easily the open coastline could have been lost to camp and caravan sites, car parks and shanty towns of beach shops and ice cream sellers. This is not to condemn these things in themselves but if they were allowed everywhere then the beauty and peace of the countryside which many people seek would vanish. The designation of Exmoor as a National Park has helped to keep it a place where people can still find refreshment for the spirit through quiet enjoyment of its natural beauty.

Much of what the Park Authority does tends to go unnoticed, at least by the general public. Once overhead electric wires have been re-routed underground there is nothing to show that the Park Authority has worked long and hard to get them moved. There are sometimes accusations that too much money is being spent. In fact the money the Government allocates to Exmoor National Park is additional money which is spent in the area and so helps boost local economic activities. The Park Authority is one of the largest employers on the moor and many people, both local and from away, are employed in a variety of full- and part-time jobs; rangers, estate workers, graphic designers, clerical support staff, planners and scientists. The local economy also benefits from contracts put out to local firms, the support of craft industries and the setting aside of land for light industry. The fact that Exmoor is a National Park also encourages visitors to come to the area and so helps the many local people who provide for tourists.

Exmoor National Park Authority, in everything it does, starts from the premise that the Exmoor landscape needs to be protected. There are still many people who don't think like that although they don't usually have views as extreme as the lady who, after visiting Exmoor, wrote this letter to the Chairman of the National Park Committee.

'While on holiday in the West Country it struck me that Exmoor looked rather barren. The idea occurred to me that a very beautiful city could be built in the middle, giving beneficial scope for many types of art in the building. Everything done by hand, with the best craftsmanship. No disturbing modern art or concrete, just sheer beauty to the eye.' The writer goes on to hope that 'the idea might become popular for other wide open spaces.'

More often people have not really thought about how a place like Exmoor survives. They do not recognise its fragility and just take it for granted, assuming that the landscape will be there for them to enjoy for ever without any effort on anybody's part. They are not aware that England has been losing an area the size of Exmoor to development every six years since the 1940s. And there are still a few people oblivious of quite basic ways of behaving in the country like leaving gates as they are found, keeping dogs under control and taking litter home. At first farmers feared that if Exmoor became a National Park an influx of visitors would bring many problems of this sort in

Red deer.

their wake. That this generally hasn't happened is due in large measure to the careful handling of potential problems by members of the Park staff.

It is because so many people have only a vague idea of what a National Park is and of the importance of its work that one of the Park Authority's most important roles is what is known as 'interpretation'. This includes helping people with the practicalities of their visit and providing information but, more importantly, is concerned with helping them understand why Exmoor is protected as a National Park and how the things being done to conserve the Exmoor environment can equally apply elsewhere. The work of the Park Authority with young people is crucial, not only in helping them to make the best use they can of the moor for study, recreation and adventure but because they are the people of the future and if the planet is to survive then they must be made aware of its fragility and the alternatives for human beings, to preserve and enhance or to exploit and destroy.

Another question that is sometimes asked is, 'Just which Exmoor are we trying to conserve?' Is it the Exmoor before John and Frederic Knight reclaimed the Royal Forest or Exmoor before the advent of the internal combustion engine? One thing that is sure is that Exmoor cannot go backwards. Every period of human activity has left its mark on the landscape whether it was the pre-historic clearing of trees, the medieval summer grazing of the Royal Forest or the ploughing of Stowey Allotment in 1977. Exmoor is not a museum to be held in a time warp. Managing woodland in traditional ways is seen as worthwhile when it makes economic as well as ecological sense. Farmers need to make a living and have to be sure that supplementing the production of food by providing for tourists while, at the same time, looking after Exmoor's landscape is going to provide them with the income they need.

Neither can Exmoor stand still. Whatever decisions and actions the Park Authority takes will have an impact on the future Exmoor landscape. In the past people often did not consider the long term consequences of their actions on their surroundings. Even now some can be singularly unaware that what they do may be contributing to the gradual destruction of the countryside. One advantage that the Park Authority planners and scientists have is a greater knowledge and understanding of the outcome of their actions and in consequence, their responsibilities are that much greater.

The Exmoor of the present day evolved naturally through its exploitation by human beings living their ordinary, everyday lives. In planning for the Exmoor of the future the Park Authority, using the knowledge, tools and techniques now at its disposal, is in the position to create the landscapes and habitats needed for the new lifestyles of the twenty-first century without jettisoning or destroying what is valued from the past.

When National Parks were first chosen the key consideration for their choice was wildness. There are areas of Exmoor that are still wild but as we have seen, disappearing wood and moor, improved roads, more motor cars and even footpath signposts and information boards have all contributed to the decline of Exmoor's wild and remote areas. The Edwards Review Panel, set up by the Countryside Commission to look at the future of National Parks, endorsed in 1991 what they saw as essential. 'The National Parks still contain the greatest tracts of open countryside, the strongest sense of remoteness and the greatest and most dramatic scenery when nature seems to be most about us.
'If an area is to merit the title *national park* these qualities must be combined over very extensive tracts of distinctive countryside which provide a sense of wildness.'

The Park Authority cannot look after Exmoor without the help and co-operation of those who live and work there and those who visit. In a recent letter to the *West Somerset Free Press* someone wrote, 'Exmoor National Park is for all of us, not just those who think it is a fixed landscape defined by dead romantic poets.' It is for all of us and we are all in some way responsible for making sure that Exmoor survives.

What will Exmoor be like in the year 2034?

Best thing that ever happened to this area was when the National Park bought four and a half thousand acres. One dreads to think what could've happened to that ground if any developers had got hold of it. Could've been planted or all sorts of things ... now all the moorland on both sides of the village belongs to the National Park and I think 'tll stay as Exmoor that way instead of being torn to bits.

Stan Curtis of Simonsbath
Retired foreman with the Fortescue Estate
Born 1927

Ranger Tim Braund with an attentive audience at Exmoor National Park Authority's Woodland Week 1994.

Acknowledgements

This book could not have been written without the help of a great number of people who have lent treasured photographs to be copied, recounted memories and supported us in innumerable ways.

We would like to thank them all and also many others whose photographs and information have, for reasons of space, not been used in this book. We hope there will be another! Thanks, too, to all those who were photographed in the 'now' pictures.

We would especially like to thank these people, listed in alphabetical order. Mrs Bailey of Carhampton for the loan of her Dunster Estates Sale catalogue; Tom Bartlett of Berrynarbor who has allowed us to use some of his encyclopaedic collection of postcards; members of the Bawden family of Cloggs Farm, Hawkridge for photographs and memories; the Bickersteth family of Gallon House Farm; Mrs Branfield of East Hollowcombe, Hawkridge; Stan and Millie Curtis of Simonsbath for photographs and memories; Barry Darch for permission to use his poem 'Larkbarrow'; Mrs J. Dymond (née Melhuish) for the photograph of tailors at Cutcombe; Gary Earl of Yeo Mill; the Exmoor Society for photographs; the editors of the *Exmoor Review* for quotations; Mrs Florence Hall for photographs and memories; Ben Halliday for permission to quote from his speech at the fortieth anniversary celebrations; Mrs Violet Haynes for her account of the Lynmouth Flood; Nigel Hester for photographs and information; George Huxtable for photographs of Shoulsbarrow; the family of Mrs Fanny Jenkins of Winsford for photographs; Mrs Greta Melhuish (née Huxtable), once of Challacombe, for memories; David Pile of Simonsbath; Porlock Museum for photographs; Postman Roger; Somerset Archive and Record Service; Victor Newton (once of Brushford) for photographs; Edward Nightingale for permission to use photographs taken by his father in the fifties; Kim Sanford of Dulverton; John Watts for photographs; the editor of the *West Somerset Free Press* for permission to copy and use the extract on p.25; West Somerset Rural Life Museum for allowing us access to their collection of photographs.

We would like to thank many members of the Exmoor National Park staff for practical help particularly Joanna Kidd, Michael Leach and David Wood for photographs, David Rabson for reading the manuscript and advice and Brian Pearce for photographs and patient support throughout the project. Thanks too to Karen Binaccioni at Westcountry Books for her design skills, Gerry Belton for constant encouragement and to Norma Deering, not only for being the enigmatic figure in many 'now' pictures but also for umpteen delicious working lunches.

Hilary Binding
Michael Deering
October 5, 1994

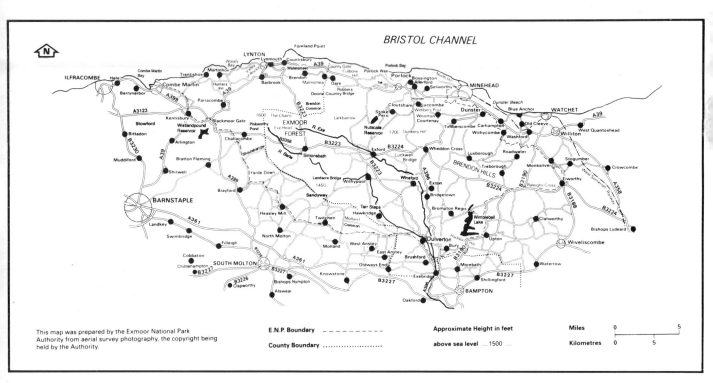

E.N.P. Boundary ─ ─ ─ ─ ─ ─ ─

County Boundary ....

Approximate Height in feet

above sea level ___ 1500 ___

Miles 0   5

Kilometres 0   5